Lazarus,
COME FORTH!

Also by John Dear

Disarming the Heart
Jean Donovan and the Call to Discipleship
Christ Is with the Poor
Our God Is Nonviolent
Oscar Romero and the Nonviolent Struggle for Justice
Seeds of Nonviolence
The God of Peace
The Sacrament of Civil Disobedience
Peace Behind Bars
Jesus the Rebel
The Sound of Listening
The Road to Peace
Living Peace
Mohandas Gandhi: Essential Writings
Mary of Nazareth, Prophet of Peace
The Questions of Jesus
Transfiguration
You Will Be My Witnesses
The Advent of Peace
A Persistent Peace
Put Down Your Sword
Daniel Berrigan: Essential Writings

Lazarus,
COME FORTH

*How Jesus Confronts the Culture of Death
and Invites Us into the New Life of Peace*

JOHN DEAR

ORBIS BOOKS
Maryknoll, New York 10545

Founded in 1970, Orbis Books endeavors to publish works that enlighten the mind, nourish the spirit, and challenge the conscience. The publishing arm of the Maryknoll Fathers and Brothers, Orbis seeks to explore the global dimensions of the Christian faith and mission, to invite dialogue with diverse cultures and religious traditions, and to serve the cause of reconciliation and peace. The books published reflect the views of their authors and do not represent the official position of the Maryknoll Society. To learn more about Maryknoll and Orbis Books, please visit our website at *www.maryknollsociety.org.*

Copyright © 2011 by John Dear
Published by Orbis Books, Box 302, Maryknoll, NY 10545-0302.
Scripture texts in this work are taken from the *New American Bible with Revised New Testament and Revised Psalms* © 1991, 1986, 1970 Confraternity of Christian Doctrine, Washington, D.C., and are used by permission of the copyright owner. All rights reserved.

Queries regarding rights and permissions should be addressed to:
Orbis Books, P.O. Box 302, Maryknoll, NY 10545-0302.

Manufactured in the United States of America

Library of Congress Cataloging-in-Publication Data
Dear, John, 1959–
    Lazarus, come forth! : how Jesus confronts the culture of death and invites us into the new life of peace / John Dear.
       p.   cm.
    ISBN 978-1-57075-936-9 (pbk.)
    1. Raising of Lazarus (Miracle)   2. Nonviolence–Biblical teaching.
    I. Title.
    BT367.R36D43 2011
    232.9'55–dc22   20110088222

For Paul Farmer,
friend and peacemaker

*I have come that they might have life
and life to the full.*
−John 10:10

I shall die, but that is all that I shall do for death.
−Edna St. Vincent Millay

*Lead me from death to life,
from falsehood to truth,
from despair to hope,
from fear to trust,
from hate to love,
from war to peace.
Let peace fill my heart.
Let peace fill my world.
Let peace fill the universe.
Amen.*

Contents

**PART III:
SERVING THE GOD OF LIFE**

INTRODUCTION

The Gospels depict Jesus engaged in a mighty struggle against death. He came, he said, to give sight to the blind, freedom to the captive, liberation to the oppressed, good news to the poor—in each case calling people to the fullness of life and to victory over the powers of death and deadness. His was a life of boundless compassion, creative nonviolence, and universal love. As we know, in his struggle against the deathly empire of his time, he gave up his own life. Yet we also know that he was raised. With an empty tomb, a cast-off shroud, he left us unmistakable signs that God had vindicated life. In this world of death and woe, he left us the promise that life yet holds a slight edge over death. There is a name for this triumph of life through loving nonviolence. We call it "resurrection."

This vindication of life over the power of death is a central theme in all four Gospels. According to the three Synoptic Gospels—Matthew, Mark, and Luke—all probably written within the space of a decade shortly before or after the destruction of Jerusalem in 70 C.E.—the critical climax of Jesus' ministry comes when he turns from his healing and preaching ministry in Galilee and heads toward Jerusalem to confront the most violent institutions of his day.

In Herod's Temple he finds the chief sign and symbol of imperial, worldly, religious, and divine power, all rolled into one. There he chastens the opportunistic religious authorities

1

in their collaboration with Rome. Driving the money-changers from the Temple, he makes a public spectacle of himself, rebuking the alliance of religion and imperial power in profiting from the poor in the name of God.

By the wisdom of his day, Jesus' journey to Jerusalem was imprudent. By stirring the vipers in their nest, he must have known the likely consequences. Nevertheless, undeterred, he upset the tables of the money-changers and scattered the Temple coins. Here was a powerful countersign, an act of what today we would call "nonviolent civil disobedience." This nonviolent Jesus was neither passive nor afraid; he was provocative, daring, public, and revolutionary. And he would not tolerate injustice anywhere.

This civil disobedience becomes the apex for the narratives of Matthew, Mark, and Luke. It is clearly the climactic moment of Jesus' life, for which he is immediately arrested and put to death by the empire.

The same story appears in the Gospel of John, an account written some thirty or forty years later. But John presents a far different order of events. He *begins* Jesus' journey with the demonstration in the Temple and has Jesus refer right there, as the angry authorities surround him, to his impending resurrection. For the culmination of his story, John chooses instead a far different episode: the famous account of the raising of Lazarus.

The raising of Lazarus is not found in any other Gospel. Traditionally presented as a demonstration of Jesus' friendship with the sisters Martha and Mary of Bethany and their brother Lazarus, it is a story that highlights his capacity for human grief and the power of faith and prayer.

But I believe it signifies much more. John's persistent theme is this: the God of life calls all human beings out of the culture of death into the fullness of life. It is a bold new view of Jesus' presence among us. Jesus, the God of life, through creative non-violence, confronts the power of death itself and calls humanity to live in the new life of resurrection, here and now. The Synoptics speak of resurrection as a *future* reality. John doesn't dispute that view. But he adds something new. For John, the promise of resurrection is also *now*. In theological parlance, he preaches a *realized eschatology*. That is to say: We can live today without fear of death. We are free to renounce it, free to confront it, free to undermine the culture built on it, free to enjoy the fullness of God's life within us and among us. Resurrection in John's account means the freedom to break the unanimity of our repeated and rabid rush toward war and all the methodologies of death. For John, Jesus is the God of life come to turn the world of death upside down.

As with all of John's stories, there is always a sense that he is nudging us, by means of signs, in the direction of a larger reality, a truth beyond simple telling. Scholars have long acknowledged that John's stories work on multiple levels: the level of the narrative and the level of allegory—a kind of collective meaning that rises off the page. With the suppleness of a poet, John turns us toward his precious discovery: *resurrection is here and now, for one and all.*

And if we are free to defy deathly institutions, we are now free to pour out our lives in service to death's victims, to offer compassion, to secure justice, to inoculate the world against its own violent ways, to beat swords into plowshares and study war no more. We are freed to live as if death has no dominion *this* side of life.

It is an audacious thesis. But on this John bases the very life of the nonviolent, life-giving Jesus. In John's Gospel, Jesus' very life bespeaks resurrection. Wherever he goes, his disarming presence leaves merciless death embarrassed and impotent. Threats and dicey situations abound, but Jesus faces them with fearlessness and truth. The downtrodden who cross his path feel better, more dignified, because here is one with not a trace of violence in him. "Jesus," Daniel Berrigan once said to me, "didn't have a mean bone in his body." His life, all said, was a life of perfect nonviolence—a life which in the end could not be contained by death. It was a risen life even before resurrection had ever occurred. And John, in his roundabout way, sets this thesis before us.

We too are summoned out of the culture of death into the way of nonviolence. All of us are called to share the risen life here and now. In John's Gospel we hear the invitation over and over: "Enter eternal life today. Do not do the works of death. I have come that you might have life and life to the full. Whoever believes in the God of life will have nothing to do with death. Live in the new freedom of love and peace!"

In chapter 11 the action reaches its peak. We hear that Jesus' friend Lazarus has died. But in this context, Lazarus is more than a friend of Jesus. According to theologian Monika Hellwig, *Lazarus represents humanity*. If this is true—and I submit that it is the key to the entire Gospel—then John has taken us into deep waters. The story of this raising is John's way of dramatizing how Jesus has come to call everyone and every culture out of the tombs of death into the new life of peace.

That is why this story is the dramatic culmination of John's Gospel. The proprietors of death—the Sadducees, the Herodians, the courtiers of Pilate, all who benefit from imperial occupation—all feel in Jesus' message a personal threat, and so they plot his demise. Death is all they know. They cannot run their empire, live off the backs of the poor, and continue to wage war if these nonviolent resisters do not fear death. So they plot to kill him.

But Jesus persists. From now on, lovers of God are free of death and its metaphors. The ruling authorities have lost their power; the sting of death is gone. Our resurrection has begun. In confronting the tomb of Lazarus, Jesus confronts every culture of death throughout history, including our own. Here begins the abolition of war. Here marks the end of greed, poverty, executions, nuclear weapons, environmental destruction, and every injustice. And it falls to us, following the example of the nonviolent Jesus, to carry on the work of life until all is fulfilled. As his followers, we are summoned to continue his story, take up his campaign, engage the culture of death through his creative nonviolence, and court resurrection by insisting on the fullness of life for one and all.

And so I offer this meditation on the raising of Lazarus as an invitation into Gospel nonviolence. My hope and prayer are that this little book will inspire us to hear anew Jesus' great command—"Lazarus, come forth!"—so that we might all leave the tombs of death and walk freely in the reality of a resurrection already realized.

The implications are rich and broad, and they brim with exciting new social, economic, religious, and political consequences. Have no fear. All of us are summoned. If we do our part for the global grassroots movement for justice and peace, then a new day of peace is truly at hand. Everyone can have a new chance to live life to the full.

May we hear the call, roll back the stone, and emerge from the world of violence into loving nonviolence. May we live life to the full in resurrection peace and welcome God's reign, here and now, for one and all.

I dedicate this book to my old college friend, Dr. Paul Farmer, who has spent his life healing the poor in Haiti and elsewhere.

I thank my friends Robert Ellsberg and Wes Howard-Brook for their comments and suggestions about the manuscript. And I especially thank my friend Ted Gordon, who proofread every word and made countless suggestions over the course of six months in 2010. A week after he sent me his last thoughts on Lazarus and resurrection, he died suddenly of a heart attack at the age of fifty-two. I give thanks to the God of life for my friend Ted who lives now in the new life of resurrection peace.

JOHN DEAR
Santa Fe, New Mexico

THE GOSPEL OF JOHN, CHAPTER 11

Now a man was ill, Lazarus from Bethany, the village of Mary and her sister Martha. Mary was the one who had anointed the Lord with perfumed oil and dried his feet with her hair; it was her brother Lazarus who was ill. So the sisters sent word to him, saying, "Master, the one you love is ill."

When Jesus heard this he said, "This illness is not to end in death, but is for the glory of God, that the Son of God may be glorified through it." Now Jesus loved Martha and her sister and Lazarus. So when he heard that he was ill, he remained for two days in the place where he was. Then after this he said to his disciples, "Let us go back to Judea."

The disciples said to him, "Rabbi, the Judeans were just trying to stone you, and you want to go back there?" Jesus answered, "Are there not twelve hours in a day? If one walks during the day, he does not stumble, because he sees the light of this world. But if one walks at night, he stumbles, because the light is not in him."

He said this, and then told them, "Our friend Lazarus is asleep, but I am going to awaken him." So the disciples said to him, "Master, if he is asleep, he will be saved." But Jesus was talking about his death, while they thought that he meant ordinary sleep. So then Jesus said to them clearly, "Lazarus has died. And I am glad for you that I was not there, that you may believe. Let us go to him." So Thomas, called Didymus, said to his fellow disciples, "Let us also go to die with him."

When Jesus arrived, he found that Lazarus had already been in the tomb for four days. Now Bethany was near Jerusalem, only about two miles away. And many of the Judeans had come to Martha and Mary to comfort them about their brother.

When Martha heard that Jesus was coming, she went to meet him; but Mary sat at home. Martha said to Jesus, "Lord, if you had been here, my brother would not have died. But even now I know that whatever you ask of God, God will give you." Jesus said to her, "Your brother will rise." Martha said to him, "I know he will rise, in the resurrection on the last day."

Jesus told her, "I am the resurrection and the life; whoever believes in me, even if he dies, will live, and everyone who lives and believes in me will never die. Do you believe this?"

She said to him, "Yes, Lord. I have come to believe that you are the Messiah, the Son of God, the one who is coming into the world." When she had said this, she went and called her sister Mary secretly, saying, "The teacher is here and is asking for you." As soon as she heard this, she rose quickly and went to him. For Jesus had not yet come into the village, but was still where Martha had met him.

So when the Judeans who were with her in the house comforting her saw Mary get up quickly and go out, they followed her, presuming that she was going to the tomb to weep there. When Mary came to where Jesus was and saw him, she fell at his feet and said to him, "Lord, if you had been here, my brother would not have died."

When Jesus saw her weeping and the Judeans who had come with her weeping, he became perturbed and deeply troubled, and said, "Where have you laid him?" They said to him, "Sir, come and see." And Jesus wept. So the Judeans said, "See how he loved him." But some of them said, "Could not the one who opened the eyes of the blind man have done something so that this man would not have died?"

So Jesus, perturbed again, came to the tomb. It was a cave, and a stone lay across it. Jesus said, "Take away the stone." Martha, the dead man's sister, said to him, "Lord, by now there will be a stench; he has been dead for four days."

Jesus said to her, "Did I not tell you that if you believe you will see the glory of God?" So they took away the stone. And Jesus raised his eyes and said, "Father, I thank you for hearing me. I know that you always hear me; but because of the crowd here I have said this, that they may believe that you sent me."

And when he had said this, he cried out in a loud voice, "Lazarus, come out!" The dead man came out, tied hand and foot with burial bands, and his face was wrapped in a cloth. So Jesus said to them, "Untie him and let him go." Now many of the Judeans who had come to Mary and seen what he had done began to believe in him.

But some of them went to the Pharisees and told them what Jesus had done. So the chief priests and the Pharisees convened the Sanhedrin and said, "What are we going to do? This man is performing many signs. If we leave him alone, all will believe in him, and the Romans will come and take away both our land and our nation."

But one of them, Caiaphas, who was high priest that year, said to them, "You know nothing, nor do you consider that it is better for you that one man should die instead of the people, so that the whole nation may not perish."

He did not say this on his own, but since he was high priest for that year, he prophesied that Jesus was going to die for the nation, and not only for the nation, but also to gather into one the dispersed children of God. So from that day on they planned to kill him.

So Jesus no longer walked about in public among the Judeans, but he left for the region near the desert, to a town called Ephraim, and there he remained with his disciples. Now the Passover of the Judeans was near, and many went up from the country to Jerusalem before Passover to purify themselves. They looked for Jesus and said to one another as they were in the temple area, "What do you think? That he will not come to the feast?" For the chief priests and the Pharisees had given orders that if anyone knew where he was, he should inform them, so that they might arrest him.

—from the New American Bible

Part I

THE GOSPEL OF LIFE

God so loved the world that God gave his only son so that everyone who believes in him might not perish but might have the fullness of life. . . . Whoever believes in the Son has eternal life, but whoever disobeys the Son will not see life. —John 3:16, 36

Whoever hears my word and believes in the One who sent me has eternal life and will not come to condemnation but has passed from death to life. —John 5:24

Amen, amen, I say to you, whoever believes has eternal life. —John 6:47

Whoever keeps my word will never see death. —John 8:51

Chapter 1

THE KINGDOM OF GOD
IS LIFE

In August 2002, I began a term as pastor of four poor parishes in remote towns of northeastern New Mexico. That September, confirmation class for the teenagers resumed, a class traditionally taught by the pastor. My friend Sister Hildegarde oversaw all the other classes. So on a Wednesday night, with a vague lesson plan in mind, I set off for Cimarron, a meager, secluded village nestled against the Sangre de Cristo Mountains.

Sangre de Cristo, the Blood of Christ—name of the ruddy range and a sign of the land's Spanish heritage. As for "Cimarron," it means "wild and unruly," refuge in the mid-1800s to storied gamblers and gunslingers. At the edge of Cimarron still stands the old "hangin' tree," where occasions of frontier justice drew in eager spectators from miles away. In the cemetery stands a time-effaced marker of a priest gunned down by a desperado.

I arrived at the church hall toward evening and met the kids for the first time. A dozen teenagers slumped around a table in the kitchen. None had come from prosperous homes; few had ever ventured outside their desert poverty.

As I took my seat among them, they turned to me with obstinate eyes. They were entering their third year of class and the novelty had long disappeared. I glanced at their workbook and had little trouble understanding why. A dull, plodding catechism on the sacraments unequal to young minds awakening to a tumultuous world.

We began with a short prayer, then we introduced ourselves. I tried to warm the chill. "So," I said, "tell me what you know. What do you know about God, the church, the sacraments? What do you know about the spiritual life?"

"We know everything," growled one of the boys, sparking smirks and titters.

Uh-oh, I thought—here's trouble. But I gathered myself and pressed on. "Well . . . what do you think of the Gospels? Have you read them?" Well, no they hadn't, they said, their eyes on the table.

I had found my entrée. Leave the workbooks at home, I told them, and I handed each a brand new Bible. This year, I announced, we will read the Gospel of Mark, line by line, beginning tonight. Then I issued an invitation. Tell me what you don't like; tell me what you like. What makes sense, and what sounds crazy? Listen to the text; I want to hear what you think.

This seemed in their eyes an adult thing to do, no more rote learning, and they perked up wonderfully. That very night we plunged in, taking turns reading aloud. From the get-go, John the Baptist made a strong impression, poor desert dweller like them, someone on the margins, making history despite long odds. His was a life that piqued their imaginations.

A few verses later, we came to Mark's central theme: "The Kingdom of God is at hand. Repent and believe the good news." What does this mean? I asked in full teacherly mode. What is this "Kingdom of God?"

A moment passed. They glanced at each other. Then one took a breath and turned my way. In his voice was something like

pity, as if my ignorance disappointed him. "The Kingdom of
God," he said with an impatient look, "is life."

The Kingdom of God is life! What? I was struck with astonish-
ment. Out of the blue a priceless insight, simple and truthful, a
flash of wisdom worthy of Thomas Merton or Thich Nhat Hanh.
It was an exhilarating moment and I was brought up short. Why
had this never occurred to me before? Perhaps I was teachable
after all!

After class, I headed home under a big moon, wending
through the desert plain along a desolate asphalt ribbon. I could
make out in the distance the shadowy forms of buffalo, elk, and
deer. And along the way I pondered the student's words. God's
reign offers fullness of life for everyone. Friend and foe, us and
them, east and west, north and south. Love and peace and joy
for one and all, here and now.

In my mind the images abounded. Laughing children, affirming parents, happy marriages. Plentiful food and bountiful wine.
Good friends and uplifting music. Peaceful days and beautiful
landscapes. Living daily in the growing awareness of God's loving, abiding presence. Meaningful service and gentle compassion toward one and all. Letting go and surrendering to God.
Dying peacefully in God's love and peace. Grace upon grace,
love upon love, peace upon peace, every day immersed in God's
good graces. Fullness of life is the reign of God—the Kingdom
of God is life. *Live it up!*

The Kingdom of Death, the Culture of Violence

A magnificent vision, as if springing from the prophets. But
a blunt survey of our world reveals another scene. The grand
vision wavers like a mirage, appears to our disbelieving eyes
utopian and absurd. Few live such richness of spirit. Most find

themselves stuck in this world and its kingdoms, stuck in our cultures of greed and violence, misery and death.

Life is hard, life is a struggle. For many, life means only death. People all over the world are stooped under the burden of hunger and war, ignorance and neglect. They flee and die under the military adventures of the superpowers and elsewhere under the terrors of tribal warlords. Many labor for little; many come to early and unjust deaths. And over us all hovers the specter of nuclear weapons and environmental destruction, both a result of a few thousand rich people spawning an epidemic of corporate greed.

To protect their global control, their "national interests," their "way of life," sleek armies march and drill all over the globe. The latest menace—the unmanned "drone"—casts its shadow over the world's poor in Gaza, Afghanistan, Pakistan, Iraq, and along the U.S.-Mexican border. Like mechanized mosquitoes, they buzz overhead taking videos and photos, and anyone not authorized by the Omniscient Computer back home, the drones are ready to bomb.

Alas, this seems to be the way of the world—a kingdom altogether different from the Kingdom of God. Call it the kingdom of death, and how hard for our transfixed minds to concede its reign. There is in the nature of deathly powers something elusive. Hectic and threatening and adroit at covering their tracks, they ensnare and overwhelm us; they exhaust our mental capacities, feeble as they often are. In biblical parlance, they possess us.

As if in a bear trap, we are caught. Nuclear weapons come off as a fact of life, and there's little that can be done about it. Our government turns a menacing eye on "enemy" after "enemy," and with the media deploying its manipulative powers, we fall into line. The gap in wealth yawns like a canyon, and we on the privileged rim chalk it up to God's preferential favor.

The big business of death seems eminently normal—even desirable. To those who would mindlessly grab, the business of death yields big returns. To the rest? Who cares about the billions of the nameless and the faceless?

Life has gone awry. And questions keep coming up. How can millions starve and we not feel it? How can the nation gear up for yet another war, and we ask no pointed questions? How is it that the Cold War is long over, and we resign ourselves, still, to nuclear arsenals? How can we carry on when the earth itself suffers from our destructive policies?

Reaching for a familiar metaphor, I offer something of an answer, an inconvenient truth: we as a people have made a social contract with death. We've made a bargain with the Devil— somewhat like this: let us be reasonably safe and prosperous and we'll rock no boats, we'll turn a blind eye toward the suffering of the poor and of creation. Buy us off; we'll go quietly along.

It is, we know, a hurtful bargain, for once we sign on, our inner light extinguishes. We plow through life thereafter in vagueness and darkness, in harness to our paycheck. We count ourselves lucky for a day off now and then, a night on the town to divert us from our depression and quiet despair. Television is our sad lot—and rote living, rote churchgoing, rote dying. We are enslaved, deadened, entombed by the culture of violence.

Kingdom of God? What might that be, and who understands? Beyond a narrowly parochial sense, we haven't a clue what "fullness of life" is.

"Pax Romana," the Way Things Were

The Way Things Are was The Way Things Were. Savagery and bitterness marred Jesus' own day. Empire was in full force, its victims the wretched of Judea and Galilee. Anyone who objected, or worse took matters into their own violent hands, such as the Zealots, was summarily executed. The Jewish aristocracy, on the other hand, jostled for the highest perches and, as Rome's surrogates, harshly administered local rule. So the people suffered doubly; they labored under the burden of two overlords, the one a vassal of the other. And both took a sizeable portion of olives and grain.

Taxes to the hilt and, as to survival, no margin for error. These indeed were violent, oppressive times. And when the peasant fell behind, the Herodian elite and priestly aristocracy were on hand with false solace. With a serpent's grin, they offered . . . credit. Credit pending appraisal of the collateral. More often than not it was the peasant's ancestral land.

Now his land turned to sinking sand. Another withered crop, another lean year, and the peasant went hopelessly in arrears. The land, his only asset, was foreclosed and conveyed to the creditor. More fertile acreage to join to the creditor's already handsome estate.

Here was a predatory investment scheme by anybody's measure, and it was open to rulers and priests. They robbed the peasants through credit *and* tithe and all manner of religious fees. Poverty, hunger, debt, and empire. Life was short.

None of this was unusual—it was the typical arrangement. Wherever Rome went they relied on the local aristocracy to make the imperial machine run without friction. By no means for the convenience of the people, but for the avarice of Rome. And for their services the ruling class was amply rewarded, namely, allowed a portion of the spoils of Pax Romana—the so-called peace that comes with empire. A false peace, as Calgacus famously said: "They create a desolation and call it peace."

It was The Way Things Were. Injustice everywhere and enigmatic forces too complex to unravel. Just as in our own times we resign ourselves and flounder, so did people in Jesus' times.

So also in John's Gospel, where the characters blink vacantly and the crowds mill about haplessly. But in John's Gospel, Jesus takes center stage and with a word or a gesture lifts the people's burden and shows them a way out of the no-win system. Put an end to injustice, withdraw cooperation with the empire, rely on murderous tactics no more, he announces. The kingdom of God is at hand. Begin eternal life right now, he says. It is God's good pleasure to give it to you. Eternal life, even now, is the will of God. Receive my gift of true peace.

In Him Was Life

John the Evangelist penned a magnificent opus to life. The God of life entered the deathly world to lead all to the fullness of life. *Fullness of life here and now.* It has taken me many years for me to understand John's central theme: "life, and life to the full."

> *In the beginning was the Word, and the Word was with God, and the Word was God. He was in the beginning with God. All things came to be through him, and without him nothing came to be. What came to be through him was life, and the life was the light of the human race. The light shines in the darkness, and the darkness has not overcome it.* (John 1:1–5)

The prologue declares that our discipleship into this life makes us "children of God." We are to enter the fullness of life and become children of the God of life. We are to renounce every trace of death, live in God's reign in peace with all humanity. That's what we were created for, that's what we are called to. More, it's the only way out of the empire of domination, control, and death.

Trouble is, when Jesus speaks to the characters in the Gospel about life, about resurrection, his words seem to evaporate before reaching their ears. No one grasps what he's saying; their imaginations falter. The same with us today. Violence seems so normal, so woven into our social fabric, Jesus' words sail over our heads.

When Jesus says to the people, for example, "The truth shall set you free," their bafflement nearly jumps from the page. "The truth shall set us free?" One can just see them frowning. "What we need is a big, bad-tempered army. An *army* shall set us free. Or perhaps a warlike messiah to establish a heavily armed rival empire. Until then, we'll lay low and play it safe."

Jesus, however, reveals a God of life and calls us to a freedom we can scarcely imagine—a life free of death, a world free of war, a new nonviolent humanity free of violence.

Soon after the prologue, John the Baptist comes on stage and speaks of this astonishing person about to come into their midst. When Jesus arrives at last, John's disciples ask him nervously, "Where are you staying?" His answer—"Come and see." It is his first summons to others to journey into the fullness of life. *Come and see*—it's his recruitment slogan. As the story unfolds, we come to understand. He invites them to forsake violence, injustice, empire, and despair and to enter into his world of creative nonviolence and unconditional love. Which is to say, fullness of life here and now, a peace not of this world.

As we turn page after page we see the nonviolent Jesus fearlessly confronting the world of death. Over the next ten chapters he performs a series of "signs" that provokes public crises, sparks heated debates, and triggers attempts on his life. We meet a cast of characters, caricatures of ourselves some of them, whom John uses to cast light on his readers' complicity with the culture of death. Each character Jesus tries to draw from the grip of death to verdant new life. And as he helps them imagine, he imagines and names his nature and role. Who does he say he is? *The Living Bread, Living Water, Light of the World, the Good Shepherd, the Resurrection, the Vine, the Way, the Truth, the Life.* Quite a piece of literature, it features poetic self-imagery, obtuse characters, public crises, and mounting death threats— a turbulent tale characterizing God's reign of life breaking into our deathly world.

The tale reaches an unparalleled climax in chapter 11, the point in the story where Jesus most daringly confronts death and its culture of violence. He calls dead Lazarus from his tomb, raises him to life, and uproots the basis of empire itself. It's an allegory of the ultimate nonviolent revolution—the resurrection of humanity into God's reign of life, a new world of justice and peace. To this advocate for peace the authorities know only one response: stamp out the insurrection before it gets out of hand. Arrest him and put him to death. He's a disturber of their brand of peace. It goes to show that the most obtuse of all are the authorities themselves. They turn like automatons to the final solution, though Jesus has shown through Lazarus that death no longer has the last word. Domination is an illusion, after all. The revolution of nonviolence known as resurrection has begun.

But before we ponder the parable of Lazarus, let's walk through John's story of Jesus through chapter 10.

Chapter 2

"I GIVE THEM ETERNAL LIFE AND THEY SHALL NEVER PERISH"

The raising of Lazarus brings the Gospel story to its highest pitch, but being in the hands of a deft storyteller, along the way we meet foreshadows, figures, omens, and signs. Two episodes begin John's Gospel. The first is the sign at the wedding in Cana. The second is Jesus' civil disobedience in the Jerusalem Temple.

In Cana, during the height of a wedding celebration, the wine runs out—a faux pas for the steward. But Jesus saves the day. On hand are vessels set aside for Jewish ritual purification, and to the servants he says: fill them with water. A hundred and eighty gallons—no small number of trips to the well. And next time the steward samples the wine, he's puzzled to find it clearer and more flavorful than before. The party goes on without pause; the revelers go on raising their glasses to the happy couple. The best wine saved for last.

A fine opening act brimming with subtle meaning. Jesus here accomplishes two things—he abolishes the need for religious cleansing rituals, and he previews God's fullness of life as a wedding celebration that goes on and on. Warmth and happiness and no end to the finest wine. What a nonviolent, life-giving Savior we have!

The next episode necessarily takes on a more militant tone, because fullness of life can't flourish without confronting deathly institutions. Jesus comes to Jerusalem and enters the Temple, and there he stages a protest against its oppressive ways. He overturns the tables of those who exchange currencies, and with a whip for directing cattle (a cord for herding, according to the Greek, not a whip for flogging) he sets the sacrificial animals loose. A deed worthy of a prophet, pregnant with subversive meaning. Indeed, the evangelist is linking in our minds Jesus with Jeremiah. Jesus has taken up his mantle and, like Jeremiah, denounces injustice, calls us back to the ways of God. It is for the reader to understand: a great prophet is in our midst.

And more than a prophet, for from the opening scenes, Jesus alludes to resurrection.

By what authority do you interfere with Temple business, the authorities and the crowds ask.

"Destroy this Temple," he returns, "and I shall rebuild it in three days."

No surprise, his words go over their heads—and ours as well. To the Gospel writer, resurrection is no mere act of resuscitation once the last breath is drawn. Resurrection implies not only a new existence in heaven but an end on earth to injustice, to greed, to oppression of the poor, to war, to empire. A vision not universally received. In response to Jesus' nonviolent resistance the authorities react predictably and clumsily. As if by blind instinct, they formulate dark plans. "Let's arrest and destroy him." What they don't understand is that they're up against the good purposes of God. And even executing Jesus won't stop his movement of justice and peace. He will rise in his followers, and justice and peace will prevail one day. Death cannot in the long run hold back fullness of life.

It's an idea that exceeds our feeble minds and is hard to understand. But our skilled storyteller helps us by introducing four characters, known in literary circles as "types." John brings them on stage to show us how we ourselves typically evade, misunderstand, or reject Jesus' summons to new life.

Might Not Perish, but Might Have Eternal Life

We meet first the fearful and complicit Nicodemus. John composed him as a Pharisee, a member of the Sanhedrin, the ruling council employed by the Roman empire to enforce its occupation. Next we meet an unnamed Samaritan woman drawing water from the ancient well of Jacob. Then a woman caught in the act of adultery facing public execution. Finally, a blind man whom Jesus heals and who, when he shows Jesus gratitude, the affronted authorities excommunicate from the Temple.

As for Nicodemus, the Gospel writer implies he should have known better. Instead, what do we see? A man who hears the rumors of Jesus' action in the Temple and who is now frightened and confounded. Nicodemus shrewdly arranges a meeting to get a handle on the man—a secret meeting under cover of darkness. The Gospel writer is tipping us off: Nicodemus lives in darkness, not "in the light."

Jesus receives him nevertheless, and the discussion begins. "You must be born from above," says Jesus. The Greek for "from above" also means "again." And confusion churns in the Pharisee's mind; he can't grasp this talk of rebirth. Grammatically it baffles him, but he also can't get hold of the spiritual and political implications. "How can one enter the womb and be born again?" A member of a powerful institution, he's long been in unholy alliance with the Roman empire and turned a blind eye toward its terrors. At the same time he's a student of the Torah, a religious elder, supposedly the epitome of godly living. But before Jesus' wisdom he flounders. He strains to understand but hasn't a clue.

Now at an impasse, the two part ways—Jesus to go on building his movement of enlightening nonviolence, Nicodemus to continue his deathly living in darkness. It is beyond Nicodemus to convert to Jesus' way of nonviolence, the way of eternal life. He can't surrender to his status as a child of God. He ruefully chooses otherwise; he remains complicit with the culture of death, whose father is Satan.

There is in Nicodemus's liberal heart some sense of the culture around him and some inclination to temper its harshness. As Jesus' trial approaches, for instance, Nicodemus admonishes his colleagues to adhere to some semblance of due process. And when that fails, he takes it upon himself to help anoint Jesus' brutalized body. But his good gestures fall short. Jesus asked of him radical discipleship—a clean break from complicity. One can't have it both ways. One can't enter fullness of life and still cling—in his case, by belonging to the Sanhedrin—to the trappings of imperial domination, and power.

God's purpose isn't domination but life, eternal life now— the purpose behind the famous words Jesus speaks to the hapless Pharisee: "For God so loved the world, he gave his only Son that everyone who believes in him might not perish but might have eternal life." In the cycle of domination, we perish. The Son shows us new life in a world without the downward spiral of violence. Such new life requires that we withdraw from all imperial aspirations and the deadly methods such aspirations employ. Eternal life requires that we live within the boundaries of nonviolence and unconditional love.

A momentous choice and Nicodemus faltered. His heart grew faint, and so does ours.

The Dead Will Hear . . . and Live

In chapter 4 we encounter another figure, an unnamed Samaritan woman. In the heat of the day she trudges to fetch water at the ancient well of Jacob. And there she meets Jesus, who engages her in the longest dialogue in all the Gospels. The two overcome formidable barriers: the cultural barrier between men and women and the other between Samaritan and Judean. He takes the initiative and shows his vulnerability; what he has yet to say to anyone else he says to her. He is the Christ, the bearer of the nature of God, who offers spirit and truth beyond borders, beyond provincialism, beyond cultures. Spirit and truth are available to all. Drink and you will live.

It is an offer that piques her interest. He offers her liberation from a narrow ethnic and national identity. She is the beloved daughter of the universal God, she now realizes, free to live in love with all her sisters and brothers. Unlike Nicodemus, she grasps the idea and then runs off to the village to tell of the man at the well "who told me all about myself."

I believe that Jesus wants to have that same spiritual/political conversation with each of us. He invites us all beyond our narrow self-understandings—that egocentric sense of ourselves based on ethnic, cultural, and national distinctions. Until these are transcended we cannot claim our true identities as sons and daughters of God. Until then, we can't very well love those outside the "tribe." Jesus calls us to a broader vision. He bids us to come alive and see everyone as a brother or sister, each one a child of God. And together live life to the full.

But to take Jesus at his word requires that we turn our backs to the culture of death. And it requires us in turn to be receptive to new possibilities—a bigger God, a worthy identity. Letting Jesus reveal himself, accepting the nonviolent God of spirit and truth, seeing ourselves as children of God, rejecting false identities the culture imposes on us—these will move us toward social and political freedom. Which is to say, above all else we'll forsake the violence of whatever culture we find ourselves in. And likely we'll run off to proclaim our new discovery. Exhilarated and hopeful we'll understand ourselves more deeply, sense our calling and direction more clearly. Every other interest will pale in comparison, and we'll want to drop everything for this chance at discipleship, this chance to join the campaign to heal and disarm our brothers and sisters, that all may enter the new country of peace.

Our next figure by which the Gospel writer teaches us is the adulteress. The authorities march into the Temple with her in tow. "Moses commanded us to stone such women," they say. "What do you say?" They're baiting Jesus to refute their authority, to hem and haw his way into blasphemy and thus break the law. One misstep on his part and they'll be able to justify a double stoning—of Jesus and the woman. But Jesus isn't so easily outsmarted; he exercises nonviolence with great creativity. First thing he does is calmly write in the sand. A delay tactic and it works. He pulls their attention to the ground and for a moment distracts them from their self-righteous anger. A space is opened up for them to hear the great commandment. In that space Jesus delivers his famous words: "Let the one without sin be the first to cast a stone."

His words transfix them, and one by one they drop their stones and slink away, the first to go the elders. They're the ones who know the law of Moses best, and they recall the ancient provision: anyone who witnesses an act of adultery will likewise be subject to death by stoning. Jesus has not only saved the woman; he saved them too!

"Let the one without sin. . . . " Jesus knows us all too well. We're all sinners. Not one of us has the integrity, the authority, to judge or condemn others, much less order their execution. The Gospel writer is telling us: the days of stoning, killing, executing—and bombing—are over. God's fullness of life requires humility, humaneness, nonviolence, and compassion.

Here Jesus grants amnesty to the woman condemned. But the meaning of the episode goes further than that. John is telling us: Jesus saves us globally from our being condemned to death, a sentence we are scarcely aware of, so accustomed we are. Nuclear stockpiles, bombing runs over poor nations, creation itself under threat. We're habituated to these. But Jesus would disarm us to walk in peace and freedom—free of the mortal sin of violence.

Hard to comprehend—for the authorities, for the disciples, and for us—even though Jesus tells us directly. "Amen, amen, I say to you, whoever keeps my word will never see death" (8:51). The woman was spared death and so were the elders. And so might we be. If we live by his teachings and example, if we practice creative nonviolence, if we resist the culture of death, we'll find ourselves on a journey of resurrection into a new realm beyond condemnation, a new world without violence. Deathly ways will no longer guide us; the reign of God will be in our midst. God's spirit of nonviolence will lead us into "fullness of life."

"Whoever hears my word and believes in the One who sent me has eternal life and will not come to condemnation but has passed from death to life," Jesus announces. "Amen, amen, I say to you, the hour is coming and is now here when the dead will

hear the voice of the Son of God, and those who hear will live."
No more talk of the "dead burying the dead." With John's Jesus,
the living live and let live. Live it up, everyone!

I Give Them Eternal Life and They Shall Never Perish

In John's chapter 9 we come to one of the most extraordinary of
all the Gospel tales, the account of the blind man. One Sabbath
day in the Temple, Jesus walks by and sees "a man born blind
from birth"—the word *anthropos* meaning not just a single
"man" but also all of "humanity." John takes us into deep water
again. He places an allegory on our hands. He's portraying the
human moral condition: we are all of us blind from birth. When
the visionary Jesus heals the blind man, he heals all of us from
darkness into the light of vision that we might see one another
and live in peace.

But Jesus' healing is not without opposition. The authorities
feel slighted and affronted and determine to discredit the man.
He's hauled before them for interrogation; after him, his parents. As for Jesus, they cast him in a disreputable light: he's a
fraud, a sinner. But the man presses back, saying a healer like
that can come only from God—an act of insubordination that
outrages them further. "And they drove him out."

Hearing of the man's excommunication, Jesus looks for him
on the outskirts of the Temple and there receives the man's worship. There, outside the Temple, the two of them cast out, Jesus
finally receives the faith he seeks—not from the dutiful religious
but the excommunicated marginalized.

In this unnamed character, we find a model, a disciple ready
to suffer and die for his allegiance to the life-giving, nonviolent
Jesus. One thinks the story was meant to encourage the struggling Johannine *agape* community. But it crosses the millennia

and strengthens us as well. Cultures of death may well reject us, but we need not fear. Put your faith in the God of life and all will be well.

John's four figures help us understand. With the stunning "I am" sayings, John takes us further into the meaning of Jesus' life. "I am," Jesus says, "the Bread of Life, the bread which comes down from heaven and gives life to the world" (6:33). It's an image that alludes to the manna in the desert, which sustained the Israelites on the cusp of starvation. "Your ancestors ate it," Jesus said, "but still they died." *Still they died*—which means in John's mystical style, they went the way of the Canaanites. Like all peoples finally, the Israelites themselves took for themselves a king and forged a covenant with death.

Which is to say, they succumbed to imperial aspirations. The Philistine menace defeated finally, the Israelites achieved sweeping dominion. And with the administration of Solomon it crested. He consolidated power by dismantling the Mosaic tribes. Territories were expropriated, tribute was exacted. Armories were built and artisans put to work turning out chariots for his standing army. He conscripted battalions of laborers, who under the lash erected marvels of architecture, including the Temple, adorned to enshroud the king in holy mists of elevation and honor—not unlike the ancient pharaoh. A bitter irony. But such is the accustomed way of empire. Its foundations are war and intrigue and, invariably, the backs of the poor.

They ate the manna, said Jesus. And still they died. But then a distinction is made, a new gift offered. "*This* is the bread," pointing to himself, "that comes down from heaven; whoever eats *this* bread will live forever."

Instead of subjugation, equality; instead of tyranny, mutuality; instead of the terrors of death, fullness of life. Jesus offers "a more excellent way." This bread, if we receive it, ends the famine of domination, greed, and violent power.

"I am the living bread that came down from heaven . . . the bread that I will give is my flesh for the life of the world." A down-to-earth soteriology. Joining his substance to ours, so to speak, makes us nonviolent children of God. Then will the world resonate with sweet life, not the discord of death. The world will become a haven of life for all.

Building this haven becomes Jesus' project. He heals the son of an official, saying, "You may go, your son will live." In Jerusalem he asks a man by the pool of Bethesda, a pool believed to heal, "Do you want to be well? Rise, take up your mat and walk." He bears the gift of new life, starts in his own day the process of resurrection. Rise, he commands. Live, he says. "Just as the Father raises the dead and gives life, so also does the Son give life to whomever he wishes." He not only foreshadows the resurrection of Lazarus, but also points to the resurrection of all who follow him.

If we follow his teachings of love, peace, and nonviolence—if we withdraw our support for imperial ways—we will escape the cycle of violence. We'll discover a fullness of life we didn't think possible. We'll enter the land of the living.

When John wrote of Jesus as the "Bread of Life," he was just beginning his list of images. He also portrayed Jesus as the "the Good Shepherd," a shepherd come so that his sheep might have "life and life to the full." The good shepherd protects the flock and, if need be, lays down his life. And the sheep in return know his voice and follow. Thieves and hirelings, the sheep keep clear of. "A thief comes only to steal and slaughter and destroy." But the good shepherd can be trusted. "I came so that they might have life and life more abundantly. . . . I give them eternal life, and they shall never perish" (10:27–28).

In the background resonates the famous psalm—that of the Good Shepherd leading the sheep toward green pastures. The figurative language runs deep. Jesus leads humanity to green pastures fenced in by nonviolence. He protects against forces of death, from any who would do harm. We are not to understand the allusion as suggesting heaven or as pointing to a numinous afterlife, but a place where the sheep might have "life to the full." A place of plenty and self-determination. And not even a place, rather a mind-set, a courageous spirit, a heart for mutuality. The pasture represents a life-affirming understanding of God. In God's name, we are free now to refuse to submit to cultural limits on our humanity. We're free to conspire to cast off our enforced mind-sets and enjoy one another in peace. The pasture means wherever life prevails.

More, the evangelist hands us a second distinction to ponder: the Good Shepherd's ways. As opposition mounts, Jesus nevertheless refuses to issue a call to arms—unlike every other faction of his day. He gathers no hidden cache of weapons. He establishes no revolutionary boot camps. Rather he defends the sheep by laying down his life—and taking it up again. This is the way, against all reason, to shatter cruel power. It is the way, paradoxically, toward fullness of life. It is the way beyond death.

And so a new shepherd is in town. And one can all but feel priestly acrimony rise. Up until now, the title of shepherd lay in their domain. Enraged, they shout, "You are out of your mind." And the episode ends with their reaching for stones. A telling reflex. It goes to show that social structures stand on foundations of death. The rulers know well the efficacy of killing.

As the story unfolds, plots against Jesus' life gather steam. In fact, throughout the religious authorities consistently show themselves shocked, scandalized, threatened. To their ears Jesus' talk sounds like blasphemy. They've so structured power that his words are manifestly illegal. And they quickly get on with their diabolical plans. Jesus submits his grievance: "You are trying to kill me, a man who has told you the truth I heard from God." They deny it even as they organize efforts to take him down.

But things for them don't always go smoothly. When the rulers send guards to haul him in, the guards linger at the fringe of the crowd and take in his words. They find themselves moved and inspired, and they refuse the order to make the arrest (7:44). Returning empty-handed, they are interrogated by the rulers. "Why did you not arrest him?"

"Never has anyone ever spoken like this," they answer.

One of the great victories of the nonviolent Jesus.

Those in the Tombs Will Come Out

Naturally enough, the authorities don't let up. As he persists in healing and proclaiming new life, the rulers turn up the heat. They interrupt, challenge, attack, try to discredit. They threaten, contradict, call him the devil. They reject a God who brings fullness of life. Their privilege and power are at stake here. If people take up this resurrection hope, it will undermine the foundation of their rule, maybe of the empire itself. He must be stopped. As for Jesus, he will not stop. To the extent that the culture stands on violence, he will stand against culture. As a consequence, for his remaining days, he will be a hunted man.

The world is drunk with violence. Jesus' entering the world is the intervention it desperately needs. Often friends confront an alcoholic, force him to recognize his addiction, urge him to renounce it, and invite him to become sober. The same with Jesus. The God of life intervenes in the world, shows us our sickness, and summons us to the sobriety of nonviolence. For God is a God of love and peace, compassion and mercy—a God who resists violence. And Jesus embodies this God.

"The hour is coming in which all who are in the tombs will hear his voice and will come out, those who have done good deeds to the resurrection of life," Jesus announces. He is determined to lead us into the new life of love and peace. He will not tolerate death in any form. Incorrigible, fearless, truthful, insistent, nonviolent, he sides with the poor and marginalized, resists the systems that bring death to people, points the way to a lifetime of peace, and expects us to follow. He tries to liberate us from slavery to violence and death. Over and over, Jesus confronts the rulers with an unbearable truth, namely, that death has no dominion, that we were created for Life, with a capital "L."

No episode better portrays this than the raising of Lazarus.

The authorities tried to stone Jesus to death in the Temple. Then they tried to assassinate him in the Bethany area of Judea. Jesus escapes, and this time, he walks back across the Jordan River to a safe, quiet place, where our story first began. He is still being hunted down by the authorities.

There, in that quiet wilderness area by the Jordan River, Jesus hears the news that one of his closest friends, Lazarus of Bethany, is dying and then has died. To his disciples Jesus says, let's go back. But they recoil in fear. Here to their minds is an unnecessary risk. Hadn't Jesus just escaped an attempt on his life there? What makes him think he'll fare better this time? But Jesus knows. As the God of life, he must confront death, so he tells his stunned disciples that he is turning around and walking right back to Judea, right back to the place where the authorities just tried to kill him. He will lead humanity from death to life, even if it means facing, once again, the empire's death squads. He will fulfill the life of *agape*, and love his friends even to the point of laying down his life if necessary.

As we arrive at chapter 11, we realize we have not made a long journey to Jerusalem, where Jesus engages in civil disobedience in the Temple. Instead, we've seen a series of subversive teachings and signs, nearly all of them causing crises and confrontations and death threats and assassination attempts on Jesus' life. Like the characters who struggle to believe Jesus' words and deeds, we too find his teachings hard to accept. We too struggle to understand who he is and what this promise of eternal life means. We too find it hard to imagine standing with him as he faces the rulers and their death squads. We do not know what resurrection is, much less what a more abundant life might feel like. We cannot grasp what it might mean to never taste or see death.

Few today appreciate this fundamental teaching. And how strange, since we live in the technologically deadliest generation of all time, in a world on the brink of "nonexistence." We of all people should understand the grip of death. Who ever needed this good news of "the fullness of life" more than us?

We've made a bargain with death, the same as the authorities in the narrative of John's Gospel. Some of us are wary of the implications of life. Others among us despair that change can happen, that nothing can be done. So what's the use of getting involved? What's the use of granting Jesus a hearing? But John's Jesus dogs us all our days. The God of life has overrun our deathly world, and his mission still stands: "I have come to bring you life, and life to the full."

Brace yourself, John announces, your resurrection is at hand.

Part II

THE RAISING OF LAZARUS

I am the way and the truth and the life. —John 14:6

Just as the Father raises the dead and gives life, so also does the Son give life to whomever he wishes. —John 5:21

The hour is coming and is now here when the dead will hear the voice of the Son of God, and those who hear will live. . . . Do not be amazed at this, because the hour is coming in which all who are in the tombs will hear his voice and will come out, those who have done good deeds to the resurrection of life. —John 5:25, 28

This is the will of my Father, that everyone who sees the Son and believes in him may have eternal life, and I shall raise him on the last day. —John 6:40

Chapter 3

"NOW A MAN WAS ILL"

Our story begins with an announcement: "Now a man was ill, Lazarus from Bethany, the village of Mary and her sister Martha." We have never heard of them until this moment. We presume that Jesus will drop everything and heal him immediately. But we also remember that the last time we were told about an ill man, who was blind—he represented humanity.

So too in this case. Long ago I heard the esteemed theologian Monika Hellwig, speaking at a theology conference, describe Lazarus as a symbol. In John's context, she said, the "man" Lazarus represents "humanity."

Humanity is sick, John is telling us artfully. The human race is ill, dying and helpless.

Then, when we hear that Lazarus has died, we know: humanity is altogether dead. The human race is lifeless, lying inside a tomb, no longer breathing, a victim of its own culture of violence and death.

A dour proposition, but its darkness provides the contrast to the "light of Christ." The darkness lifts the meaning of the nonviolent Jesus to exponential heights. The raising of Lazarus as parable portrays the God of life coming into the world of death and leading humanity out of its tomb into the new life of resurrection peace. Now we know why John ends his Gospel with this climactic act of liberation and resurrection.

Mary and Martha of Bethany

Lazarus was apparently one of Jesus' closest friends. His name, diminutive from the Hebrew "Eleazer," means "God helps." But according to scripture scholar Wes Howard-Brook, John's use of this priestly name may be subversive. With Lazarus's death, John might be referring to the death of the non-Jerusalem priesthood, the indigenous priesthood that the religious elite in Jerusalem had been trying to repress since Jeroboam first led people away from Jerusalem nine centuries earlier. It may also refer to the death of the violent priestly tradition of the sons of Aaron: Eleazar and then Phinehas (see, e.g., Numbers 25 and 1 Maccabees 2).

Lazarus and his sisters Mary and Martha live not far from Jerusalem, in the village of Bethany. One imagines that they often offered Jesus a place of respite from the road, a place of friendship, support, food, and warmth.

Their names come up in the Gospel of Luke (10:38–42). Jesus stops at their house in Bethany. And Mary, all ears, famously sits down at his feet, while Martha prepares things in the kitchen. Martha complains: "Lord, do you not care that my sister has left me by myself to do the serving? Tell her to get up and help me. I'm doing all the work."

And we recall Jesus' response. "Martha, Martha, you are anxious and worried about many things," Jesus answers. "Only one thing is necessary. Mary has chosen the better part, and it will not be taken from her."

For two millennia, churchmen have explained this as a story about the tension between the active and contemplative lives.

"Baloney!" says Sister Joan Chittister. "It is pure revolution." Women were not allowed to sit among men and forbidden to sit at the feet of a holy religious leader. Martha wasn't put out or inconvenienced; she was mortified, scandalized. Her sister violated custom and tradition. What if word got around?

But Jesus isn't fazed. He welcomes Mary to join in. He not only lets her sit at his feet, like any of his male disciples, he says she has chosen the better part and it will not be taken from her. Jesus, the revolutionary feminist, defends her place among the men.

How honorable of Jesus; how brave of Mary. Jesus' teachings intrigue her, this liberating talk of fullness of life and peace. Her heart soars at his words, and she gathers the courage to pull in close. And as for Jesus, no surprise that the Holy One who leads us from the ways of oppression and death would welcome a woman to listen. Of course he regards women as equals. The fullness of life is for all, for women as well as for men. One only hopes that Martha left the kitchen and broke through the male establishment—and her own fear—to sit next to her sister at the feet of the Master.

Back in John's Gospel, we are told that this same Mary is the one who anoints "the Lord" with myrrh and wipes his feet dry with her hair. When Judas grumbles about the cost, Jesus rebukes him: "Leave her alone, she bought it for the day of my burial." This episode happens later, in chapter 12, but John presumes we know the rest of the story already! The tale of Lazarus's death and resurrection must be read within the context of Jesus' own death and resurrection. Jesus' raising the dead man, his beckoning humanity into life, will cost Jesus his own. And, presumably, in some measure, ours as well.

For now, Jesus abides across the Jordan River. He has just escaped an assassination attempt in Bethany, and word has come that his friend Lazarus is sick, and then dead. We note that the message comes with few details. In the Greek, it reads: "The one whom you are friends with is sick." Scripture scholar Wes Howard-Brook notes that it bears the anonymous tone of an underground movement, where messages are necessarily cryptic. No names, no details, lest the message fall into wrong hands. The secrecy hints of a guarded network of a subversive community.

The message arrives, and we the readers expect one of two things. Jesus will stay put because Judea's death squads had just recently tried to kill him and still have orders to kill him. Or he will head to Bethany with haste and keep Lazarus from dying. Neither happens. Rather he lingers by the Jordan then announces to his disciples: let's head back to Bethany. By then two days have passed.

For the Glory of God

"This illness is not to end in death, but is for the glory of God, that the Son of God may be glorified through it," Jesus tells them. He "loved Martha and her sister and Lazarus," we're told, and "remained for two days in the place where he was." Then he said to his disciples, "Let us go back to Judea." Up until now we haven't known that Lazarus's illness was critical. Nor do we have any sense of what the glory of God means, nor how an illness might glorify the "Son of God." Each word adds to our confusion.

In the original Greek are added connotations to help us understand. "The one you love is ill," the sisters report. Of the many Greek words for love, here they use *philia*, meaning "the love between friends." When in John's Gospel Jesus speaks of love, he employs the extraordinary word *agape*, meaning extravagant, unconditional, sacrificial, universal, nonviolent love—the love that lays down one's life for one's friends. How hard for us to understand, but Jesus held his three friends in an embrace of *agape*—the larger meaning being: Jesus so loved them he laid down his life for them. Jesus will come to practice what he preaches. He loves Lazarus; he loves humanity. He will risk his life for Lazarus—and humanity.

Still, why does Jesus dawdle for two days while his friend grows sicker by the minute? His answer has something to do with the glory of God and the glorification of the Son of God, this Jesus.

"Glory" nowadays comes with winning the Oscar or an Olympic gold medal or election to high office. But the reader of the Gospel will soon learn. The glory of God comes through nonviolently resisting empire and its idols, even unto death. God bestows glory on those who enact perfect *agape* for humanity. For *agape* and nonviolent resistance are the way to resurrection—John's metaphor for fullness of life—and resurrection is the ultimate glorification of the Son of God.

The Gospel gives us no clue as to whether the disciples are acquainted with Lazarus and his sisters. But they are quite acquainted with the dangers lurking in Bethany, on the other side of the river. "Rabbi, the Judeans were just trying to stone you, and you want to go back there?" We can imagine the urgency in their voices: "Are you crazy? Are you trying to get yourself killed?"

Why are they afraid? Because they do not want to get killed! They want no part of the perils he would face again in Bethany. "Let *us* go. . . . " he says. They say, "Rabbi . . . are *you* going . . . ?" The clash of pronouns tells much. They still do not grasp Jesus' fierce determination to confront death on every front. They are afraid—for Jesus, perhaps, but mainly for themselves.

We do well to pause for a moment and notice how like them we are. We have many fears, and, surely, the prospect of assassination would terrify any one of us.

Jesus, on the other hand, does not let fear rule his life. He feels it, we presume, but acts against it. He does so because he trusts his beloved God. He believes in the power of life. He knows that doing what is right—acting in truth, resisting injustice, loving his friends, practicing nonviolence—will set him free to enter, from this moment, the richness of eternal life.

"Are there not twelve hours in a day?" Jesus asks them. "If one walks during the day, he does not stumble, because he sees the light of this world. But if one walks at night, he stumbles, because the light is not in him." Here he continues an oration from an earlier episode, just before he healed the blind man (in chapter 9). Then he had said: "We have to do the works of the one who sent me while it is day. Night is coming when no one can work. While I am in the world, I am the light of the world" (9:4–5). The point is: let Jesus be our light. As long as we live in his light, we shall see our way forward even in the darkness on the path to new life. He is our way out of the culture of death, out of the tombs, into the culture of life, God's reign of peace.

Our Friend Lazarus

Finally, in a poetic turn of phrase, Jesus tells them, "Our friend Lazarus is asleep but I am going to awaken him." The disciples, always obtuse, get confused and get it wrong. "If he is asleep, he will be saved." "Saved" here does not mean our popular concept of "salvation"—dying in grace and going to heaven. It means here to be made well. The Gospel writer lays stress on their gaffe. "Jesus was talking about his death, while they thought Jesus meant ordinary sleep." Their dullness forces him to speak in terms more prosaic. "Lazarus has died. And I am glad for you that I was not there, that you may believe. Let us go to him."

Our friend Lazarus. . . . Lazarus, we learn finally, is their friend too! For Jesus, friendship forms the basis of the fullness of life. We read later: "There is no greater love than to lay down one's life for one's friends." And at the last supper, he says: "I no longer call you slaves, but friends." It slowly dawns on us. Jesus is a God of love and peace who wants to be our friend. And if we hang in with the story to its fullest conclusion, the realization pierces our defenses. In Jesus, God seeks friendship with humanity. God sees the whole human race as God's dear friend. Reverting to the allegory, Jesus' returning to raise his friend carries the mystery of God turning the divine gaze in friendship to help entombed humanity.

Sad to say, friendship has fallen out of fashion these days. Our lives are so busy and complicated we have little energy to make new friends. More than that, friendship is no longer a part of our model of life. We don't see life anymore as a journey together with others, or even with God. Our culture fragments. Young people fall into isolation, caught up as they are in the culture's competitive rat race. They fall into the traps of alcohol, drugs, random sex, militarism, and the pursuit of money—all of these destructive of community and friendship. Often even the church fails to encourage friendship. It rather puts people in their places and strongly implies: stay put or be ostracized. Or in extreme cases, expelled.

What are you willing to do for your friends? Jesus asks the fearful disciples. Are you willing to risk your lives for Lazarus? As I am for humanity?

The question hangs in the air, awaiting our response. Need it be added, conventional wisdom offers a ready reply. A stentorian No. The wise thing is to watch out for number one. Take care of our own. Our culture forces us into a cloud of cynicism, coldness, judgmentalism. Though we're part of humanity, we've by and large forsaken it. We carry a few loved ones in our hearts—our spouses, children, relatives, a handful of friends. We may—at our rare best—lay down our lives for a spouse or a child. But for a friend, not so likely. For the human race? Not in our wildest dreams. At bottom, we think none too highly of human beings. I've spoken to many young people around the world, and they confide in me a seismic shift: the welfare of humanity isn't worth the effort. Humanity exhibits little awareness, little gratitude, little self-criticism, little learning from their mistakes. Many young people would rather expend their energies on behalf of animals and the earth. At least the earth, when it's cared for, returns the favor by flourishing with verdant life. At least the dark watery eyes of animals express their quiet thanks.

Still, the best among us have proven that befriending humanity is possible. They've proven that giving our lives for the other—for humanity itself—is our highest calling. Nelson Mandela, for instance. He languished twenty-seven years in a narrow cell in South Africa. And all because of his single-minded desire to end apartheid and rebuild a reconciled society. Dorothy Day is another example. For nearly fifty years she lived with the homeless and pressed New York's bureaucracies to do right by them. Time and again, she also protested our wars and weapons. Most of all, we see the love of humanity among our martyrs: from Franz Jägerstätter, the Austrian farmer whom the Third Reich beheaded for refusing Hitler's conscription, to Martin Luther King Jr., who took an assassin's bullet for resisting racism, poverty, and war.

The best among us show us. Willingness to give our lives for others exemplifies the fullness of life, the fullness of humanity— a gold standard that springs from Jesus himself. He modeled the highest of human callings. "Our friend Lazarus.... Let us go . . ."

Then he adds, *I am glad for you that I was not there.* . . .We balk at the words; they grate against our sensibilities. But there was something in Jesus' thinking along these lines: "Afterwards, when Lazarus has been raised, perhaps then they will understand." God isn't an angry, provincial God but a universal God of resurrection and life. Perhaps his disciples would learn to believe. Here, for Jesus, was something worth hoping for, and the prospect made him *glad*, the only moment in his public life he uses the word.

Such an elaborate plan makes us realize, of course, that in the believing department, the disciples must have constantly been falling short. The sticking point is their fear, which prevents their practice of *agape* for their friends. The idea of walking into the jurisdiction of Bethany, even for the noblest of reasons, terrifies them. They hem and haw. They rationalize. "He's just sleeping; a few more days and he'll probably be fine. More importantly, you just escaped an attempt on your life. Better stay away from that place. Lazarus will be saved, right?"

Not a trace of *agape* among them; they don't seem particularly glad. And when news finally comes down that Lazarus is dead, they calculate again. "Why bother now? Nothing can be done. You can make no difference now. Don't bother trying; it isn't worth the risk." Through the lens of John's allegory, John shows us our own cynicism, fear, despair, and faithlessness. "Things are too hard, societies too intractable. Let's be smart and take no risks. Let's take care of our own and play it safe.

You can only do so much." The genius of John, he speaks on two levels at once.

On the level of the narrative, Jesus is undeterred. "Let us go to him," he says. He wants this chance to reveal the God of resurrection and life, a chance to glorify the Son of God. His hour is coming. And he sees it happening, the day his disciples will believe and follow his example. And even beyond that, a day when all humanity will take up his way of nonviolence and love. Not only will they be raised, they'll transform their culture of death into a culture of life. He leaves for Bethany filled with hope. He goes rejoicing.

Doubting Thomas

Here at this moment of decision, one of the disciples speaks up, Thomas, called Didymus, whom we've never heard of before. He says, "Let us also go to die with him."

Thomas makes two other appearances in the Gospel. A few days from now, he will interrupt Jesus during his last supper discourse and ask, "Master, we do not know where you are going; how can we know the way?" (14:5). "I am the way and the truth and the life," Jesus tells him. Then, after Jesus' resurrection, when the ten other remaining disciples tell him they have seen the risen Lord, he refuses to believe.

In both cases, he's easy to reprove. When he hears about Jesus' resurrection, I think he wants to believe, but can't. The implications are too grand; they bear too heavily on his mind. He requires proof. "Unless I see the mark of the nails in his hands and put my finger into the nail marks and put my hand into his side, I will not believe" (John 20:25).But resurrection comes by way of a cross—a sticking point. Another sticking point—it turns our presumptions of culture upside down. And we recoil like Thomas. Thus Jesus offers him proof. "Touch my wounds . . . and believe."

Touch and believe; the two go hand in hand. We meet the risen Jesus when we touch the wounds of the world—the wounds of the poor, the wounds of the suffering. No one comes to believe meaningfully in the possibilities—for peace, justice, for the fruits of resurrection—until he or she touches the wounds of the world's crucified peoples. Without that, our believing reeks of sanctimony, hypocrisy, and religiosity.

Through our work among the homeless, in soup kitchens and shelters, through our work with the sick and dying, our work among migrants and prisoners, our work in war zones and refugee camps, our work in our broken inner cities, whenever we meet the poor, disenfranchised, and marginalized, when we touch their wounds—their pain, their suffering—we meet the risen Christ. We discover God. And this encounter not only gives us new life and hope; it changes our lives. It fills us with new life and sets us on a journey to peace, even to the cross of nonviolent resistance and beyond to resurrection.

This is a consistent Gospel pattern. Once you encounter the risen Christ by touching his wounds in the world's poor, you find yourself on a route different than you had planned. Thereafter you're likely to speak up, to advocate for justice, to accept being embroiled in legal trouble. Christ rises in you, and you begin a new resurrection life.

And soon the Gospel life takes on a political mystique—the doubting Thomas episode makes this clear. He sees, he touches. And now believing, he utters his first subversive words. "My Lord and my God"—the same title, word for word, demanded by Domitian, emperor from 81 to 96 C.E., the generation in which John wrote. Any other claimant to the title—and his followers—was suspected of treason and subject to arrest and execution.

Thomas then comes under a new light. His doubts had less to do with mere cognizance of facts than with their implications. Belief requires conversion and response. And Thomas responds. He embraces his future, which consists now of nonviolent resistance to the brutal empire. If necessary, to the point of martyrdom.

But I jump ahead. Here in chapter 11, Jesus says to his (male) disciples, "Let us go to Lazarus," this even if death squads are patrolling for him. And this is when Thomas nobly lifts his voice. "Let us go and die with him."

On the face of it, how brave he is! Finally, a disciple willing to shoulder the same risks as Jesus, ready to be identified with the Holy One—the strongest support offered by any of the male disciples in the four Gospels.

But wait. What happens? Thereafter, they're nowhere to be found. They never appear in the rest of the story! We hear nothing of them again until verse 54—long after the story has ended and Jesus has gotten himself again safely to their desert hideout.

I submit that, in the end, they stay put in relative safety, and Jesus goes to Bethany alone.

Thomas and the male disciples say the right things, but can't get their feet to move. They are all talk, but they do not walk the walk. When push comes to shove, when the discipleship journey must finally begin, they're nowhere to be seen.

In Thomas, we see ourselves. This is the habit of many churchmen today. We heap our praises on Jesus, lift our prayers up to him, say we'll follow. But facing death is another matter. We don't lift a finger in the effort to end war, disarm our nation, dismantle our nuclear arsenal, or abolish poverty. Civil disobedience in the style of Gandhi and King lies quite off the map.

Where are our ministers, priests, and bishops in the struggle for justice, disarmament, and peace, against the many guises of death? They're nowhere to be seen. They're not part of the story. Jesus walks alone.

Chapter 4

"I AM THE RESURRECTION AND THE LIFE"

Jesus returns to Bethany, alone and unarmed, entering a region where, if the authorities can avoid arousing a public outcry, they will seize this subversive and deal with him in the standard way. Notwithstanding the dangers, he goes in a spirit of perfect mindfulness, nonviolence, and peace. He remains centered in the God of life, who calls him "My Beloved." That abiding sense of God's love, whatever happens, keeps him from succumbing to worry, anger, or fear. That is the secret to his daring nonviolence.

Few of us attain such peaceableness. Not many reach such heights of composure and poise. Small disruptions throw us off. How easily we anger, grow anxious and judgmental. Mindfulness eludes us; our normal mental state is scattered mindlessness. The violence on television only feeds our agitation. Wounds still fester from the violence of our earliest years. And the unending series of vicious crimes and wars preys on our minds. Our routine each day pulls us this way and that, and so hectic are our days that rarely do we feel at peace. But here we read of Jesus, mindful and at peace, though he knows that the death squads are out there and have their instructions.

How does he do that? How does he embody such peace? His every step is peaceful. His mind rests in truth. His heart is filled with unconditional love. He takes in awareness with every breath. And he can do it because he knows who he is. Close to his heart and mind lies his awareness that he is the beloved of God whose personal gift is true peace. He is free to trust, and as he enters a perilous region, he has reason to be glad. God will be glorified; perhaps his disciples will believe. At any rate, he knows to whom he belongs; his life is complete. He belongs to his beloved God, and he knows that, in the long run, all will be well. And so he is centered and mindful. Jesus embodies peace.

Because he knows he belongs to the God of peace, Jesus is inspired to practice active nonviolence in the face of violence. It is what draws him forward into the dangerous terrain. Where mercy is involved, he's undeterred. He goes to liberate Lazarus or, in the broader sense, to liberate us all. Nothing passive or disingenuous about it at all. He shows himself as direct and fearless; he intends, despite the certainty of affronting the authorities, to challenge the pretensions of death. And the pretensions of the rulers, who wield coercion like a sword. Jesus' plans are laid out, and he'll see them through.

Anyone who claims to be Jesus' follower is assigned the very same task. Not only are we to reorder our lives toward peaceableness and mindfulness, we're summoned to go farther and challenge our culture of war—this for the liberation of everyone everywhere. We too are summoned to undertake that journey of peace and nonviolence on behalf of humanity.

It's an arresting image of Jesus that John portrays—the nonviolent Jesus on the road, marching, campaigning, vulnerable, prepared to face the very crowd that tried once already to do away with him, eager to help his friend, determined to liberate humanity from the culture of death. This brave Jesus seeks people to join his peace movement. He wants followers who will walk with him. And so the story serves as more than a story. It carries something of an invitation.

We're invited—you and I and everyone. Jesus invites us to follow his example, to join his campaign. We can do this, because John's Jesus is trustworthy; we know in our bones that he's right. If we journey with him and bear his spirit of love, nonviolence, and mindfulness, we'll find our lives bathed in blessings and meaning. More, we'll reach a critical mass, create a global grassroots movement of nonviolence, and change the world.

"Join my long walk to Bethany," the nonviolent Jesus says, "my cosmic Selma march to liberate humanity from death. I promise you the fullness of life."

The People of the Culture of Death

Bethany is but two miles from the big city. A short jog from the local seat of power, the rulers and their retainers and the acquiescent crowds. And now, at the passing of Lazarus, a crowd gathers around his tomb. They've arrived to begin the ritual thirty days of mourning, to "comfort" Martha and Mary.

Who are these who have come to aid and comfort? The very ones who had earlier tried to put Jesus to death! Killers when the occasion calls for it, but now "professional mourners," rocking from the waist, weeping and keening, fulfilling their religious obligation. It's a scene that bespeaks a kind of schizophrenia. Though Lazarus's death evokes public sorrow, in their hearts lies a spirit of murder. The sick man dies and by rote the crowd sheds tears. But the One most alive comes under the crowd's evil eye. Tears notwithstanding, they are servants of death because they still stand poised to do death's bidding.

Meantime, they go by the book and honor the time-honored traditions. Model citizens, all of them—public servants, abiders by the law, devotees of the Temple. But inwardly, they're jealous, greedy, violent—bound by the shady spirit of power and empire, prepared to crush all who threaten their lucrative domination over society. Good people by all appearances, on hand to grieve with the grieving, but to their dark minds there are some they deem expendable. Those who rock the boat deserve to die. Despite its cultivated image, the crowd, to use modern jargon, is not "pro-life."

Little today has changed. We too mourn our dead, yet we scarcely pay heed to our culture of death. We too call ourselves "pro-life," but there are always exceptions. Deep down, we too believe some are expendable.

We see this discrepancy most sharply in our scripted public grief for the young who die in Iraq and Afghanistan—moments of silence are observed, flags lowered—even as we cheer the war on and pony up large tax liabilities to keep it going. We grieve for our dead and yet urge our young to join the military and its killing spree.

In recent years our government has not allowed the media to bring images of the hundreds of caskets into our living rooms. It doesn't want any true grief, the kind that might lead to a new spirit of compassion, that might sap our energy for war and create a movement to stop the killing. The culture allows the pretense of grief, enough to keep the wars going, "to honor the dead." So the military chaplain blesses the body and the war, a distant bugler plays Taps, we place our hand over our heart, we weep as the twenty-one shots are fired, we watch as the folded flag is given to the widow. That is all that is permitted. No questions can be asked. Public grief must be controlled, manipulated, used for the big business of war. The media, an arm of the war machine, goes right along.

So we read of the mourners at Bethany, weeping on one hand, plotting Jesus' execution on the other. And the scene raises challenging questions. Do we fulfill our churchly obligations yet turn a blind eye as the state executes another convict, the nation bombs distant civilians, and our nuclear laboratories churn out their latest weapons of mass destruction? How might we move from serving death to following the nonviolent Jesus? How can we align our hearts with the Gospel vision of humanity? In other words, how might we foster nonviolent hearts, nonviolent lives, and nonviolent cultures? How much do we truly grieve for those who have died, for the millions who die from war and poverty, and how can we renounce our cooperation with the culture of death that kills the world's poor and leads others to grieve?

The Jesus who walks alone to Bethany shows the way. Namely, we are to side with the victims, walk to where the culture of death goes unchallenged, and be emissaries on behalf of life. We can grieve for those who have died, but not as "professional mourners." Like him, we take action to make sure that no one else dies from our culture's wars and greed, that no one else has to grieve for the innocent victims of state-sponsored violence. If we trust in the God of life and love, then we can follow him on that path and lead others beyond grief, false and true, to new life and real hope.

"Lord, If You Had Been Here"

Jesus arrives at last and learns that Lazarus has been in the tomb now for four days. The soul, according to Jewish tradition, leaves the body after three days. Now it has been four; Lazarus is hopelessly gone. The pall in the air is heavy. Jesus gets no greeting from Mary—she prefers to stay at home—and Martha meets him with something like recrimination on her lips: "Lord, if you had been here, my brother would not have died."

Her desperate plea sounds all too familiar. We too cry out to Christ in utter disappointment. "If you had been here"

- My loved one would not have died.

- War in Iraq would have been averted (and in Vietnam, Afghanistan, and Central America).

- You might have protected us on 9/11.

- Nuclear weapons, corrupt corporations, crime in the cities, death row, global warming, NAFTA, the ever-widening gulf in wealth—all this could have been avoided.

- People might have lived, we might have lived.

"But you are slow to help. Where were you when we needed you."

If we survey the world and then our own hearts, we'll find Martha's despair to be our own. But we avoid looking; we are passive. Our despair runs so deep, we do not even voice it, as Martha does. As violence tears apart the human race, we scarcely take notice anymore and fail to act. Hardly a surprise then that violence comes back to haunt us. Violence upon violence leads to further violence. It's proverbial: what goes around comes around. If we fail to break the cycle, violence like a boomerang will come back to strike us. The cycle is our doing, not God's. Injustice, violence, empire, and war—the Gospel insists these are not the will of God. It is we who abide the violence of culture. We cannot justly blame God. But deep down we do.

Our despair before Christ derives not from an impassive God but our lack of faith. Somehow we haven't been able to trust in Christ's manifest ways of love, nonviolence, compassion, and justice. At church we offer our rote prayers, ignorant of the price Jesus pays in reaching out to us. And not only the price he pays but the Way he offers. Out of love he takes his chances and asks the same of us. But we do not trust Christ or God. Instead of thanking Jesus for coming to us, we complain bitterly like Martha. Instead of noticing how he walks into a mob of death squads to stand with us, we focus, like Martha, only on ourselves.

What should we say to Jesus? We should realize that he always has our best interests in mind, that he only wants to help us, that he is always helping us, and that he is worthy of our trust. He would never hurt us or do anything against us. Our first, most fitting response should be gratitude: for his taking the initiative, for risking his life to side with us, for showing us the way, for standing with us, for becoming our way.

"If you had been here," Martha blurted. Then she realizes her gaffe. Quickly she regroups and takes another tack: "Even now, I know that whatever you ask of God, God will give you."

Another big mistake. She presses Jesus to pray, even tells him how to do it. In an instant she moves from disappointment to bossiness. She has yet to learn how to sit attentively at his feet and listen, as Mary did in Luke's Gospel. Instead, she makes Jesus listen to her. So far, Martha hasn't let him get in a word.

John is deftly composing another figure, Martha, who models our behavior. I think back on my prayer life in the mid-1980s. Reporting to my spiritual director in 1990, I told her proudly of my regular morning meditation. "Every day I forcefully demand that God put an end to the war in Central America and an end to nuclear weapons. I angrily chide God for not being here to help us, and tell God in no uncertain terms what to do," I said. Finally, Sister Jane Ferdon, my exasperated spiritual director, looked at me and asked: "Is that how you talk to someone you love?" That moment, for me, was a breakthrough.

All of us are prone to lash out at God for letting us down. And we're none too shy about telling God to do what we say. Our impulse, since the foundation of the world, has been to control God to do our will. Our doing *God's* will lies quite off the map. Follow the way of Jesus? We would rather try to compel Jesus to pray as *we* want, to do as *we* want. Few of us want to listen to Jesus, much less do God's will. And so we do all the talking; he can't get a word in edgewise.

The saints tell us that prayer is formal time for our lifelong relationship with our beloved God, with Jesus. During our daily meditation, we learn to sit at the feet of the one we love and listen attentively. Over time, we can sit and rest in silence. We adore our beloved God, and enter a mutual relationship of nonviolent love. That journey begins with contemplative listening, nonviolent love, and abiding trust, no matter what.

Your Brother Will Rise

It goes against reason, but it's good that Jesus ignores our manipulations and tantrums. So habituated we are to the ways of death and war that little do we realize how weak our faith is in the God of life and peace. Jesus, on the other hand, developed perfect faith, and so he can stand before us patiently and with compassion as we rail blindly at God at the way things are. One is astonished to observe his compassion toward Martha. There is no hint of rebuke, chastisement, or ridicule. He listens with compassion—a precious blessing. For, finally, it is God's patience that disarms us and begins the process of healing and faith. Jesus takes her seriously and, in the end, tries to hearten her. "Your brother will rise."

An intrepid promise by any measure: *your brother will rise!* What does that mean? I wonder if, in our common dullness, many of us have pondered this declaration and let it sink in. *Your brother will rise.* Can we fathom how revolutionary these words are? They point to an astonishing view of reality: despite its haughty presumptions, death will not be permitted the last word. Humanity and its cultures will rise to new life. Life in the end will edge out death.

We hear notions like this at Christian funerals. Are they religious prattle? Or do we believe it? Do we expect our friends and colleagues, all who went before us, to live on in some realm of peace? Do we imagine that the untold billions who've ever lived reside now in some new realm of joyful life? If yes, then our belief should mightily bear on our lives today. It should provoke a radical shift away from the culture of death. It should guide us into the freedom to love and serve humanity—without any fear or recourse to violence. Our belief in resurrection should liberate us to live life and serve life and help others into that eternal space of peace, love, and joy, and so resist the culture of death.

Your brother will rise: The first words of Jesus, when at last Martha gives him space to speak, are words of hope. We've imagined already in good Ignatian style Jesus' lonely pilgrimage of nonviolence back toward the dangers of Bethany. Now let's imagine him before us and hear his words—*your brother will rise*—and let his hope take root in us and dispel our despair and complacency.

You brother will rise, Jesus says to each one of us. *Your sister will rise. Your father will rise, your mother will rise, your friends will rise. All will rise,* Jesus says.

We stand there dumbfounded, mouths hanging open. Our options for understanding are few. Either Jesus is mad—unlikely or we would have forgotten him long ago—or something new is upon us. The challenge is to take him at his astonishing word. That is the beginning of hope and new life. Indeed, that is the beginning of our own resurrections. Listen to Jesus, trust him, and accept his promise. If we do, then we have embarked into the fullness of life.

Martha hears and concedes, but with a hint of resignation in her words. "I know he will rise in the resurrection on the last day." Vague notions of resurrection are already in the air. Daniel of the Hebrew Bible, the writings of the Maccabees—they entertained ideas of resurrection a century or so before Jesus arrived on the scene. More, perhaps Jesus deliberated his own ideas among his friends. At any rate, for Martha, the idea of resurrection carries little energy. She imagines it as a distant and incomprehensible dream, certainly of no comfort to her in her present distress. She doesn't reject Jesus' promise; neither does she quite embrace it. She does not reject Jesus or scorn his talk. She grudgingly admits: "Yes . . . on the last day."

Who among us hasn't felt this way? At those moments of horrid news—the death of a loved one, tragic disasters, terrorism, starvation, and war—we keep from going under by repeating the mantra: "On the last day they will rise." We try to remember. We steel our wills. But in our bones we know: the last day is a long way off. Cold comfort when we live in the frightful here and the dreadful now.

I Am the Resurrection and the Life.
Whoever Believes In Me Will Never Die.

Jesus, however, knows something we do not know. The last day has come and gone! We are now in the first days of resurrection!

We have already entered upon eternal life. It begins today, here and now. Death no longer has any sway. Jesus belittles it; he compares it with sleep. Jesus knows Lazarus will rise. And death, as it were, will die. And Jesus wants us to trust in this. To trust in it like second nature—which is why he told Nicodemus he must be born from above. Trusting in resurrection requires a new kind of person, —one who renounces death as a methodology. And who does this naturally? It has to be as if by a second birth. For Jesus, such faith, such hope, such promise comes naturally. He wants us to believe naturally too. He wants us to know that with him the day of resurrection has arrived!

Martha's bleak resignation reaches his ears, and Jesus presses back. You don't understand, Martha. Hope is more immediate than you think. Today is the day after the last day.

"I am the resurrection and the life."

Here, we have the Gospel in one sentence, a truth so deep that we must return to it daily, let it sink in, listen to it, and take it to heart. Jesus is resurrection, Jesus is life, and so, the non-violent, compassionate Jesus is our hope. Our only hope.

Once again, John places the name of God from the book of Exodus in the mouth of Jesus.

"Who," asks Moses, "shall I say sent me?"

"Tell them 'I Am' sent you." "I am the One who is, the One who lives, the One whom death can't destroy."

"I am . . . ," says Jesus.

"I am the resurrection and the life. Whoever believes in me, even if he dies, will live, and everyone who lives and believes in me will never die."

In other words, "whoever is alive here and now and believes in me as the fullness of life, love, and peace and follows my way of living life, loving everyone, and confronting death, will never die, because that person lives in me and I live in that person and so that person is already in eternal life, the fullness of resurrection life and peace."

Jesus, the Gospel announces, is the God of life in our midst. He embodies resurrection and life, he is the giver of resurrection and life, he is the path to resurrection and life. He does not speak of the "Last Day," like Martha. He speaks about the here and now, about living today as if death has no authority, as if you are already in the fullness of resurrection life. With this announcement, we're free today to withdraw our cooperation from war-making, consumerism, scapegoating, weapons development, every pursuit and aspiration that makes our culture more deadly—what I've been calling the culture of death. We renounce violence, and let it go. We let his life, love, and peace live within us, so that we walk in his spirit of nonviolence. Eternal life has begun, he proclaims, you are already risen. Resist the culture of death; trust in the God of life. Live and let live.

I am the resurrection and the life. Startling and hopeful—one of the loftiest sentences in the Bible.

But what follows is nothing less than a direct challenge not only to Martha, but to each one of us: *Do you believe this?*

Well, do we? The question admits of no cheap answers. We again might pause and imagine him saying it to you and to me. Do we believe in resurrection and life, in the God of resurrection and life, in Jesus as the Way to resurrection and life? What does life mean for us? How much power do we give to death? What does resurrection mean for us? Do we believe that as we non-cooperate with death and live fully in the God of life, we will never die? And if we do believe, how do we demonstrate our trust in the God of life in a world given over to the power of death?

John's unwritten hope is that all his readers will say, "Yes, Lord Jesus Christ, I believe that you are the resurrection and the life. I believe that you have deprived death of the last word.

I believe in the fullness of life here and now, that I too can reject the culture's violent ways and become like you, a person of non-violence, *agape,* and peace. From now on, I'll serve life and resist the forces of death. You've shown us how to do it; I believe you'll see us through to the fullness of life for all." Between the lines lie John's fondest hopes.

Lo and behold, Martha believes! Or so she says. "Yes, Lord, I have come to believe that you are the Messiah, the Son of God, the one who is coming into the world." No waffling in her words, they're bold, confident, and assured. None of the male disciples in John's Gospel has spoken so boldly. The only other such declaration comes in chapter 9, from the man born blind. For John, the model believer and disciple is a woman.

But on closer look, we discern in Martha a hint of evasion. She never actually says, "I believe you're the resurrection and the life." She says, "I believe you are the Messiah . . . ," the very same words Peter utters in the Synoptics. Trouble is, Peter in the Synoptics hopes for a messianic revolutionary, one armed to the teeth, ready to take on the empire. A person, in other words, still using the means and methods of death. A violent Christ.

But no, says Jesus. He's a nonviolent messiah, a suffering servant willing to die, to give his life that all might live in the fullness of life. Not the news Peter had hoped to hear, and the squabble ends with Jesus issuing a strong rebuke. "Get behind me, Satan."

That John identifies Martha with Simon Peter should raise an alarm. First we might wonder, as Joan Chittister does, why Jesus doesn't offer Martha the "keys to the kingdom," as he does Peter in the book of Matthew. By the same token John casts doubt on the quality of Martha's faith. She offers three affirmations: "Jesus is the Messiah. The Son of God. The One coming into the world." Not bad. She goes farther in understanding than nearly every character in the Gospels. But here's the sticking point: how to believe he's the resurrection and the life? She can't quite provide Jesus the response he seeks.

Another reason to doubt the perfection of Martha's faith is that, without rhyme or reason, off she goes. She fetches her sister, saying falsely, "The teacher is asking for you." It seems the anxiety grew too hot. Too much to take in. Her nerves were shot; she had to flee. Some scholars wonder if she is merely protecting the wanted Jesus by speaking of him anonymously as a teacher. I suspect this talk of "resurrection and life" is simply too much to bear.

Martha's failure is meant to teach us. We must try to listen deeply to Jesus and let his question linger. "I am the resurrection and the life. Do you believe this?" We must take the time, sit with the doubt, live with the question. As we stay with it, we can live our way into the answer, into faith, into action. As we listen, we can try to say what Martha could not: "Yes, Jesus, I believe you are the resurrection and the life. And so I will live life to the full from now on. I will not cooperate with the culture of death. I will live in the resurrection from now on, and so be with you who are my life, my hope, my resurrection, my peace, my joy, my God."

Unlike Martha, we need not run away from Jesus. We need not complain to him, challenge him, control him, or fear him. If we take Jesus at his word and know that he is our resurrection and life, then all will be well. Our deepest desire will be to sit at his feet, take in his wisdom, and dwell in his peace. We know that from now on we will live, which means we will have nothing to do with death.

From now on we're free—of fear, violence, and death, come what may. Jesus, our resurrection and life, is with us.

Chapter 5

"AND JESUS WEPT"

"Yes, Lord, I believe . . . ," confesses Martha, affirming Jesus as Peter does in the Synoptic Gospels. But while she asserts a measure of faith, Jesus' talk of resurrection capsizes her sense of order, and she comes undone. If she had believed, she would have clung to his side. She would have prostrated herself in worship, as did the man born blind. But what does she do? She turns on her heels and flees back to town—or in allegorical terms, flees for refuge to the familiar culture where death prevails. There she feels more at home.

Meditating on the story in good Ignatian practice, one might appropriately ask: How does Jesus feel about her abandoning him? Take a moment to engage your imagination. Does she leave him feeling betrayed? Angry? Confused? Annoyed? I imagine him feeling hurt. Rejection from nefarious authorities would be no surprise: they've rejected him all along. Nor is it much of a surprise that he endures tepid acceptance from the disciples, all of them obtuse men. But not rejection from one of his closest friends. That, I imagine, is why he stands there, some distance from the village, almost as if at a loss. Martha's abrupt departure leaves him disappointed. He is crestfallen, and he needs time. He needs it for the inevitable struggle to remain centered and at peace. He must keep from yielding to despair or grief or anger. Time is needed, and he takes it to shore up his trust in his beloved God—and his broken friends.

Here is a painful vignette, and it carries a basic lesson. When the Spirit of Jesus pierces our defenses and compels us to peer into the murky unknown, don't run away. Scholars call such an experience "precritical," that is, an experience in which we haven't the reasoning capacity yet to understand or sort out. Still, we must trust and stay with Jesus, come what may. Trust in his being the resurrection and the life, for each individually and for all. We can trust him. In the crosswinds that often blow in contemplation, where up seems like down and down up, listen and remain peaceful. Let Jesus lead us though we're disoriented for a time. Stay in his presence, trust in his peace, and let love lead to worship.

Here disorientation has befallen Martha. She's hit with a kind of spiritual vertigo, and she betrays it by breaking off the discussion and running off to town. "Mary," she calls, "the teacher is here and is asking for you." She's right on the first account but not on the second. She's saying in effect: *You go meet him; it's your turn to deal with him for awhile.* And we notice, too, she has changed her tune and given Jesus something of a demotion. No longer the Messiah or the Son of God, let alone the resurrection and the life. Now he is just "Teacher," a respectful title as far as it goes, but not one requiring radical conversion and faithful commitment. Her disorientation has overwhelmed her; she flees to familiar terrain and to the predictability of Mary.

In the original Greek, we are told that Mary "rose" and went to him. Narrative criticism, as we're doing here, assumes that the Gospel writers use no word casually. "Rose" here is chosen deliberately, a word full of resonances. It suggests a big transformation. Presently for Lazarus, but imminently for Mary. Not only will Lazarus be raised, but in a sense she will too. She arises, walks from the culture of death, and heads toward the God of life. We recall Mary's sister, Martha. She took the opposite route: away from life toward the bleak "comforts" of the threadbare culture of death.

The mourners see Mary go and assume she's going to the tomb to weep, not knowing that she's rising. And they "follow" her, a word that implies discipleship. She is their teacher. In John's world of allegory, they head off with her thinking she is taking them deeper into death, literally, to the tomb itself.

Discipleship into the Culture of Death

Mary has yet to hear what Jesus has told Martha: that he is the resurrection and the life. Would she immediately believe it? Not likely, for when she gets to the edge of town, she utters Martha's very same cry of disappointment. "Lord, if you had been here, my brother would not have died." Hopelessness and despair all over again. It seems she too is on intimate terms with the power of death, convinced like everyone in town: death is lord; nothing can be done.

So far, no sign of her rising. She seems as squarely stuck in the presumptions of death as everyone else. She echoes the voice of utter hopelessness. But to her credit, she keeps her bearings. She does engage him, and she tells him how she feels. More, she falls at his feet—a profound gesture of intimacy.

Throughout, Jesus maintains a laconic silence. Here he is standing before a despairing and doubtful friend sobbing at his feet, and a keening crowd who not long ago had tried to kill him. And there he stands: steady, self-possessed, nonviolent, and compassionate. He longs for true worship. Not hero worship, not the people's projections of nobility onto him. Rather his desire is that they account God's way of nonviolence as worthy and embrace it with joy. To worship Jesus is to follow his way and to unleash a godsend of security, forbearance, and peace.

But there is little worship among the crowd. Jesus remains composed and centered, nonetheless. He does not get flustered; he does not press. Everything he does is for Mary's benefit, and Martha's and ours. He is the Mount Everest of life. Immovable, unshakeable, a rock.

It is here we see the trajectory of Mary's rising begin. There at his feet she feels his healing peace. She doesn't understand him but she begins to trust him—this contrary to the social pressure of the crowd around her that refuses to believe. She was at his feet once before as she listened to him teaching. She lies at his feet now in tears of grief. She will soon bathe his feet with fragrant and costly nard and dry them with her hair. She knows his feet well.

This latter episode, of Mary perfuming his feet, marks something of an inner change for Mary. Shortly, after he raises Lazarus, Jesus will be in Bethany again, this time during a Passover charged with resurrection celebration. Her perfuming his feet publicly displays her honor and love. And perhaps her sorrow for her slowness of heart. At any rate, her costly outlay manifests her hard-won understanding. She understands all of a sudden something of the paschal mystery. She quietly appreciates that he must return to Jerusalem. Against common sense, he must return to the culture of death and there risk martyrdom. "Leave her alone," says Jesus as Judas objects to the cost. "She bought the perfume so that she might keep it for the day of my burial." Mary has come to realize that this is the way.

Finally, a disciple who understands and will brace him in his hard choices. Mary of Bethany is on a journey of resurrection with Jesus. She moves from darkness to awareness, doubt to faith, despair to hope. No longer is she confounded by the idea of Jesus' journey to the cross and new life. She understands: it's been the way of life since the foundation of time. And she'll support him as he takes his path.

But what about now, at this terrible moment as she lies at his feet hysterical and the mourners at a distance raising a din? How does Jesus feel? We're told plainly. He was "perturbed," "deeply troubled." Rarely do the Gospel writers bother to describe Jesus' feelings. But here John tells us. Jesus is in anguish, in great turmoil.

And out of his distress, he engages for the first time the people who had previously tried to do away with him. "Where," he asks, "have you laid him?"

A cause for delight among them, one would think. Hewing, still, the allegorical line, we can all but see their thoughts. Finally, they think, he'll concede the primacy of death, and submit to our rulers, who employ it so well. He'll fall into line, and his chatter of resurrection and life will at last come to an end. He wants to see where Lazarus is laid. We'll be happy to show him Lazarus's tomb, where humanity lies dead.

"Come and see," they say with a serpent's lisp.

Come and see—these are the very words of invitation that open the Gospel. Come and see, Jesus had said to a pair of John's disciples who, following close, wanted to know where he lived (1:39).

Come and see. From Jesus' mouth these are gentle words that invite us to resurrection and new life. They call each of us into radical discipleship in the culture of nonviolence. But in the mouth of the mourners, his own words are used against him. As if they would recruit him into their culture of violence and death!

Mythically one can imagine the scene. Their spiraling eyes are mesmerizing. "Come and see the power of death! Come and see: death does get the final word. That's why we do its bidding.

Come and see: the place of doubt, despair, domination, empire. Learn the ways of death. Become a disciple of violence. See and believe in death!"

Their tone foreshadows the propaganda and seduction to come millennia later in the Third Reich.

"Before death, the hope of resurrection is all but fantasy and futility. Put an end to this talk about resurrection and life. Submit to our ways. Behold the preeminence of death!"

In ways subtle and flagrant, you and I hear this very summons every day. On all sides we are badgered to believe in the efficacy of death. War, killings, executions, bombing raids, unmanned drones, handguns, nuclear weapons, consuming more than you can afford, corporations unleashed from any and all restrictions—these, the message is, will benefit and save us.

And we go along complacently, some of us eagerly. Thirty wars rage across the globe today, a billion people starving, some twenty thousand nuclear weapons across the world, violence done in the name of law, the earth on the brink of catastrophic climate change—all this and we've scarcely anything to say. We ride the stiff current like driftwood. Even those who would register an objection feel powerless. Death lords over us, saying it has the last word. What hope can we sustain against it? The idea of transformation seems almost laughable. Relying on nothing but our own resources we quickly give in. And the minute we do we become unwitting disciples—no longer to the God of life but to the culture of death.

Each of us from our toddling days has been recruited into the culture of death. We've signed on, done our basic training, put strict limits on our consciences, and obediently fallen into line as foot soldiers of imperial aspirations. Discipleship exceeds our comprehension, even among churchfolk. New life and nonviolence baffle us. We can't imagine John's hope of resurrection, what it might mean today in practice. We've all made peace with the presumptions of death; we're used to them. We are, in fact, quite contented with the ways of death, thank you very much.

The glory of death—come and see, we tell one another. And indeed we do. Images of soldiers are displayed everywhere as icons. Sleek weapons are proudly unveiled at arms bazaars. On TV, the eerie green glow illumines the night over Baghdad, and we sit riveted before America's magnificent displays of shock and awe.

Alas, we don't know the harm our worship of death inflicts on our souls. The more we succumb, the less our chances to envision the possibilities of resurrection life. The human task of disarming our world, and our own hearts, falls beyond us. Our capacities for objecting to such things as starvation or drone warfare or nuclear deterrence get beyond our reach. All because we've internalized violence. We've delivered our souls to the spirit of empire. What we serve, in sociological terms, are systems of death. In biblical terms, we worship idols. In terms of John's Gospel, in quiet desperation we hang around the tombs. And to our dark minds there's no way out. We have internalized the culture's violence. The empire possesses us.

At our best, we Christians complain to Jesus. We have no understanding of our own man-made predicament. We have rejected his invitation to new life and have been happily recruited into the culture of death. We find ourselves perplexed about his talk of resurrection, life, nonviolence, and peace, and try instead to recruit the God of life into our violent ways of death.

Everyone Believes in Death, No One Believes in Life

How does this make Jesus feel? This question opens up new insights into discipleship and life. If Jesus is the God of life, as the Gospel of John insists, then our focus should be on him. We have only the four Gospels as guidebooks for our discipleship, so we need to stay with them, read them daily, make them part of our lives. Over time, our daily Gospel study puts Jesus at the center of our day-to-day attention. In our psychologically aware culture, we place high value on feelings. But Christians rarely consider how, in the Gospels, Jesus feels. I believe if we want to know Jesus more and more intimately, we need to ask how he feels about what is happening to him in every Gospel episode. We need to stop clinging narcissistically to our own piteous feelings and join our hearts with his. In this, yet another time of testing, the question arises: How might Jesus feel toward the crowd's counterinvitation and recruitment into the culture of death?

He is devastated.

The next verse, famous for its brevity, the shortest in the New Testament, sums it up: "And Jesus wept."

The crowd imagines they have him reduced. At last he's behaving according to cultural norms, showing his helplessness and bereavement before the face of death. Finally, he acts like a disciple. He's one of us. He's been recruited into the culture of death.

When Jesus weeps, the professional mourners, the Judeans, everyone in the crowd, shake their heads in wonder. "See how he loved him!" they murmur among themselves. Love, that is, in the brotherly sense—*philia*.

Others of a more vicious disposition offer him something like taunts: "Could not the one who opened the eyes of the blind man have done something . . . ?" Even within the boundaries of their own religious duty to mourn, they show no compassion for the weeping Jesus. "If only he had done something!" they say. This taunt recurs in all four Gospels and follows him to his last day. There, in his hour of agony and abandonment, the religious leaders and passers-by shake their heads in disbelief. "If you are the Son of God, show it, prove it. Come down from your cross." Poor Jesus. He shows compassion to everyone. Few show compassion to him.

Nobody believes in Jesus. Everybody puts their faith ultimately in the power of death.

This even though Jesus offers good news. He comes with the gift of life. He invites us to the fullness of life. He stands with the God of life, as the God of life, inviting us into eternal life beginning this very moment. He tells us that we are no longer captives of death. We can be free of empire, of oppression, of war. We need not kill or hurt one another. We can learn how to care for one another, even so far as to love our enemies. We can all live in mutuality and peace. This is God's will, and it's truly possible. But the crowd rejects his invitation. We prefer death. "We don't want resurrection or life. Come and see how effective are our ways of death. . . . "

How does this make Jesus feel?

Jesus weeps—*but not because Lazarus has died!* And not because he is powerless in the face of death. We've misread this text for centuries. Jesus weeps because everyone in the scene— the crowds, the rulers, his male disciples, even Mary and Martha—have gone only so far with him. In the end they reject his invitation to life and put their trust instead in the tyranny of death.

Earlier Jesus told us that he rejoices—he is glad—at the news of Lazarus's death. Maybe, Jesus thinks, just maybe, we will come to believe in him. Instead, Jesus finds everyone given over to the power of death. And he breaks down crying. For centuries, we have presumed that Jesus wept because of Lazarus's death and his own powerlessness in the face of death. We have passed on the legacy of the professional mourners who fulfill the religious obligation to mourn yet support the culture's infliction of death upon the poor. We have become like them, and continued their mistaken assessment of Jesus.

We've all missed the point. Jesus does not weep because Lazarus has died. Jesus weeps because everyone in the story—and all of us—believe not in the God of life but in the culture of death.

He weeps not because his friend is dead, but because all around him faith, hope, and love have died.

He weeps not because he is powerless before death, but because we have rejected the power of life.

He weeps not because his offer of life is impotent, but because we do not want it. We are quite comfortable with the culture of death. We are used to war, violence, killing, and the possibility of nuclear destruction. We know it well; we've grown used to it. We don't want any changes.

All of us, like the characters in the story, at one point or another, have thrown up our hands and said, "I'm sorry, Jesus, there's nothing that can be done. You gave it a good try, but death after all does get the final word. We're all but powerless. There is no hope. Lazarus is dead, humanity is dead, the world cannot be disarmed and changed. So let's get along as best we can. You might as well join us and make peace with the culture of death."

At this Jesus weeps.

But the story refuses to end there. Here, at the nadir of grief and apparent failure, when he hits rock bottom, Jesus acts!

The hour of resurrection has arrived.

Chapter 6

"JESUS APPROACHED THE TOMB"

Like a good dramatist, the Gospel writer leads us to the very brink of tragedy. The body now four days in the grave; the soul vacated; all faith and hope are lost. And all the characters are persuaded: death is invincible. But to the contrary, precisely here the story takes flight. Jesus, abandoned by all, takes matters in hand and clips death's wings. The presumptions of the culture are about to expire. At this moment of total despair, Jesus takes action!

"Jesus approached the tomb."

Here's a verse we can ponder for the rest of our lives.

By no means is it enough to read the words. We must put our imaginations to work. See the nonviolent Jesus, before the great maw of death, take his first steps. He has been weeping; he is in great turmoil. What will he do?

The sisters and the mourners from the city hang back, astonished no doubt. To their minds his talk of being the resurrection and the life evaporate before the reality of death. Such talk, now, has little meaning. And at any rate, the tomb is no place for a good Judean or Galilean. They wouldn't be caught dead at one; it would violate their cleanliness laws. And what's more repugnant to our sensibilities than a rotting corpse in a cavernous tomb? Still, he approaches.

He goes because he lives in an enlightened reality. It's his privilege to see that war must submit to peace, violence must submit to nonviolence, fear must submit to love. More mythically put, resurrection is stronger than entombment in our culture of death.

The God of life will be triumphant over death. And Jesus, in this moment, will enact this triumph. As the resurrection and the life he faces the reality of death fearlessly, peacefully, directly. With resurrection and life, all things are possible.

Jesus approached the tomb. Alone, unarmed, vulnerable, weak, peaceable, loving, faithful, hopeful. The nonviolent Jesus confronts the culture of death head on. He does not shy away or run away from death. He faces it and takes action.

One of the most astonishing, hopeful images of history. From it other such images have multiplied. Think of the Chinese student standing alone before the column of tanks in Beijing's Tiananmen Square. It was on June 5, 1989, the day after the government cracked down on student agitation for government reforms. The young man stood there alone, unarmed, in the middle of the street, showing himself fearless and determined. The lead tank veered one way and so did he. It veered the other way and so did he. The tank driver was baffled, the tank in effect disarmed. The footage goes down as one of the twentieth century's most celebrated images.

What became of the student no one knows. Some think he is hiding from the deathly powers he embarrassed. Most think he was arrested and whisked away secretly to face execution. Whatever his fate, his action symbolized the best of creative, nonviolent resistance against the forces of death. A modern-day

Jesus approaching the tomb, he put his body on the line and exposed the state's reliance on killing.

We might recall, too, Gandhi's nonviolent followers who on May 21, 1930, marched toward the Dharasana salt mines. Another instance of Jesus approaching the tomb. Some twenty-five hundred had trained in Gandhi's way of *satyagraha; satyagrahis* they were called. And they had resolved to come to the water's edge and gather salt and thereby symbolically break Britain's monopoly on India's natural resource. It was also an early step in the struggle for Indian self-determination.

The British seized Gandhi the night before as a kind of pre-emptive arrest, but the marchers proceeded undeterred. They would nonviolently "assault" the salt mine, Britain's largest manufacturing center.

In front of the gates, Indian guards in service to the British clutched steel truncheons, and every grade-school child knows what happened next. As the marchers arrived, the guards struck fiercely. Skulls were fractured and shoulders broken. Imagine the people's mindfulness as, despite the blows, the column pressed forward. Thirteen hundred crumpled to the ground and in the end four died. But not one raised a hand in retaliation. Not one fled as they faced possible death. Each mirrored the nonviolent Jesus as he approached the tomb.

The macabre scene was reported live by United Press correspondent Webb Miller, and news of it went around the world. And in the time it took to read about it, the myth of Britain's paternal benevolence was shattered. The marchers exposed British cruelty. It was a turning point in the struggle to bring about Britain's departure.

And think as well of Dr. King on Good Friday 1963. He and Ralph Abernathy walked into Ingram Park in Birmingham, Alabama, where they faced the simmering hostility of Sheriff Bull

Connor. It was the spring that thousands marched nonviolently for an end to segregation and faced water canons and police dogs trained to snarl and bite. The jails in Birmingham were full; the prisoners crowding the cells languished. City leaders were determined: no inroads were to be made in their fair city. Dr. King walked into Birmingham's culture of death. And on Good Friday the situation looked particularly bleak. Hundreds were in jail, and though King had promised bail, his funds were all but gone. And more, from a local court came the injunction: no more demonstrations permitted. The movement was on the verge of collapsing.

This was months before King's "I Have a Dream" speech, months before scoring civil rights legislation, and more than a year before his winning the Nobel Peace Prize. Meantime, Birmingham was bound and determined. They would yield not an inch.

King arrived and convened at the Gaston Motel with his staff and other church leaders, and the arguing heated up. They were stuck. If they folded, Jim Crow would declare victory. If the demonstrations proceeded, Birmingham had finagled the legal clout now to all but crush the movement. King later recalled, "A sense of doom pervaded the room." It seemed nothing could be done. Either way the cause was lost.

King was "deeply troubled," says historian David Garrow. Troubled like Jesus before him. And at the height of the squabbling he arose, retired to another room, and prayed. Thirty minutes later he emerged, no longer wearing ministerial black but a new set of denims. His meaning was clear. "I've got to march," he told his astonished colleagues. He decided to risk arrest, prison, even his life. As for his friends, they thought: here is the end of the movement.

And so off they went, King and Abernathy and fifty others, from the Sixth Avenue Zion Baptist Church to Birmingham's city hall. They managed four blocks before the police, in none too gentle of a mood, raced to the crowd and lurched to a stop. Film footage shows on officer seizing King by the rear of his belt and hurling him into the side of the van. Off they hauled him to solitary confinement, where he spent "the longest, most frustrating and bewildering hours I have ever lived."

But again we know what happened. His imprisonment inspired New Yorkers to raise an enormous sum and local activists to mobilize hundreds of school children. These would make up the next wave of marchers to court arrest.

As for King, he neither despaired, nor did he squander his time. He penned on scraps of paper a letter admonishing his brother clergymen, a missive known famously today as "The Letter from the Birmingham Jail." And finally when he emerged from jail he was in a stronger position to negotiate with the city the right to vote and an end to segregation. August of that same year he came to Washington and declared, "I have a dream. . . . " And not long after that he attended the ceremony at which President Johnson signed civil rights legislation into law.

But none of that was apparent on Good Friday 1963. All he could foresee was arrest and jail. And in southern towns where due process applied to people of lighter hues, he reasonably understood his chances of being murdered. Still, he took action. Peacefully, mindfully he headed toward downtown Birmingham, yet another image akin to Jesus' approaching the tomb.

There have been many times I myself have faced arrest for civil disobedience, often against war and nuclear weapons, and I well know the feeling: the beautiful and terrible steps toward the tomb. The first time for me was toward the Pentagon. The police arrested me for blocking a doorway. It wasn't so much the sit-in that I remember but the slow, mindful walk in the early morning toward the massive, lifeless building. It was on April 17, 1984, under a leaden gray sky and with a chill in the air. The weather fit my mood. I was tense and nervous and a little scared. Yet I was determined after two years of struggling to witness for peace to take my stand. The more centered and peaceful I became the surer became my steps. When I finally arrived, my heart was ready. I sat down, obstructed the doorway, and read from the Gospels. As they hauled me away I prayed for disarmament. For me a whole new beginning.

I recall, as well, walking on to the Concord Naval Weapons Station in California, where friends and I approached the base's nuclear bunkers. In my book *Peace behind Bars*, I've written about the scary morning of December 7, 1993, when I stepped illegally onto the Seymour Johnson Air Force Base in Goldsboro, North Carolina, knowing that trespassers could be shot on sight. We walked through the woods, waded across a creek, trudged up a hill, and then found ourselves right in the middle of thousands of soldiers conducting war games on an airfield of F15 nuclear fighter bombers. It was a vivid experience of Jesus approaching the tomb.

Each year to mark Hiroshima, friends and I walk from Ashley Pond in downtown Los Alamos—where the original Hiroshima bomb was built—toward the entrance of the national laboratories, busy designing bigger and better nuclear weapons. I try to make the journey in a spirit of mindfulness, aware of each step, centered in each breath, present to God's gift of peace. Each time, I recall the unarmed, mindful Jesus as he approached the culture of death. I want to carry on his legacy, to imitate his daring action, to model his fearless confrontation of death. We do not know the outcome of our actions, but we know that as his followers, we too are free to approach the tomb.

Truth be told, it's scary, this walk toward the tomb. There's a reason we don't undertake that walk. We deny the reality of death. We do not admit that we are embedded in the culture of death. We rarely even think about our own approaching deaths. So to walk toward the culture of death, to those places where death has become big business—think of arms manufacturers—where many make a fortune planning the deaths of others, is to face reality head on. It means staring death in its own monstrous face.

Jesus did this in a spirit of love, truth, nonviolence, mindfulness, and faith. He trusted in the God of life and realized his calling to be the resurrection and the life. As his followers, we are called to be people of resurrection and life, which means, at some point, we too must approach the tomb. We too need to face the culture of death.

At last Jesus reaches the tomb and stands before it. Jesus—the God of life—issues three commandments. Throughout the Hebrew Bible, this God has already commanded us: "Thou shalt not kill!" "Beat your swords into plowshares!" "Love your enemies!"

Now, in John's climactic moment, Jesus gives three new commands that overturn the tables of the culture of death.

Take away the stone! Lazarus, come forth! Unbind him and let him go free!

These commandments, if we obey them, have the power to disarm the world.

Like it or not, the God of life confronts our culture of death.

The moment of resurrection has come.

Chapter 7

THE FIRST COMMANDMENT: "TAKE AWAY THE STONE!"

There, before the tomb, Jesus commands, *"Take away the stone!"*
Astonishing words. *You want us to do what*?

Does he intend to exhume the body? Or open an inquest like a coroner? Why take away the stone? What good can come from that?

According to the Gospel writer's sustained allegory, Lazarus represents us all, entombed in a deathly culture—now as then. Imperial aspirations, nuclear weapons, corporate greed—these cause the vulnerable great harm—and ourselves as well: economically, psychologically, and spiritually. We're dead as a doornail. But then his astounding commandment: "Take away the stone!" The God of life has intervened in our common mortuary. God does not leave us for dead but takes initiative to rescue and save. And, more, to prove that death doesn't get the last word. The commandment issues like a thunderclap.

Take away the stone!

I hear these words as one of the fundamental commandments of the New Testament. Jesus, the God of resurrection and life, breaks into death's domain, where death runs amok, where the big business of death has co-opted our societies, where death cheapens life for us all.

79

Roll back the stone from where humanity lies dead, the nonviolent Jesus commands. The God of life is here.

I urge Christians to hear this commandment as never before and begin to obey. We do well to ponder our life journeys and reflect on when we've obeyed or how we might begin. Can we locate in ourselves a glimmer of desire to see resurrection and life prevail? Have we ever been astonished by an instance of death-defying, life-giving action? Where in our world is such a thing happening? How might we contribute? Imagine joining such efforts communally, nationally, globally, those campaigns that take away the stone in front of our culture of war and injustice.

If this parable points to the presence of the God of life in the world of death, then this moment sums up God's desire for the world. God will not let us stay entombed. God grapples against the culture of death. God has come to shatter the culture of death into slivers and shards and set things right that all might live life to the full.

We might have to poke in the crannies of history, but there have been many occasions through the centuries when indeed the stone has been rolled away—this just when the culture said, "Impossible."

Over the last two hundred years, the struggle has included the Abolitionists, the Suffragists, Gandhi's *satyagrahis*, Dr. King's civil rights movement, plus noble efforts to abolish apartheid in South Africa. When the moment seemed most hopeless and bleak, that's when, against all reason, society transformed. The stone budged. Yes, wars persist and our nation continues to update nuclear weapons at the design table, but we've seen as well people of intractable good will confront cultures of death.

A dramatic display occurred in the Philippines in the mid-1980s. Dictator Ferdinand Marcos had rampaged and oppressed for twenty years, sending opponents and dissenters to early graves. But in 1983, the popular exiled Senator Benigno Aquino challenged him for election. As Aquino returned from exile on August 21, 1983, Marcos's soldiers assassinated him, literally as he stepped off the plane. Rarely has a dictator shown himself so brazen. But Aquino's widow Corazon took up her husband's mantle and in his stead ran against the dictator and won.

But a dictator willing to assassinate a political opponent has no intention of stepping from power. Election results notwithstanding, Marcos proclaimed *himself* the winner.

Aquino responded by calling the people to engage in nonviolent rallies, marches, vigils, and civil disobedience. What the rest of the world did not know was that during the previous year, church activists throughout the country had held hundreds of workshops on active nonviolence. Hundreds of thousands had been trained. When it came time to roll away the stone, they were ready.

Enormous crowds took to the streets under the name of People Power Movement. Marcos in turn responded predictably, surprising no one. He ordered his military to attack the "rebels." Soldiers fanned out but were met by hundreds of thousands singing and praying the rosary. Leading them were hundreds of determined nuns in full habit, prepared to give their lives for the people's freedom. Within hours, the crowds in the street surged to three million. Fighter planes dispatched to bomb rebel headquarters found the place surrounded by huge crowds, and the pilots, with no stomach for wanton killing, saw Marcos for what he was and defected to Aquino. A dictator's nightmare. Increasingly soldiers and generals refused to train their guns on unarmed demonstrators, and the dictator soon realized his power to terrorize had come to an end.

He packed his bags and fled Malacanang Palace.

Corazon Aquino was hailed as the new president of the Philippines.

It was a four-day affair. Between February 22 and February 25, 1986, the people joined together and rolled away the stone, let light in the tomb, and ended a dictatorship. Such a thing, even a week earlier, would have been deemed impossible. But it happened. Nonviolent resistance to the culture of dictatorship and death works. Indeed, it's the only practical path toward life. *Take away the stone!*

Over the last five decades, two-thirds of the human race has been involved in nonviolent grassroots movements for positive social change. Millions, perhaps billions, have responded to the command to take away the stone. We could point to a few well-known movements. In Asia, we see the Dalai Lama's movement for a free Tibet; Aung San Suu Kyi's campaign in Burma; Thich Nhat Hanh's engaged Buddhism in Vietnam; Maha Ghosananda's peace walks in Cambodia; Sulak Sivaraksa's nonviolent struggles in Thailand; pro-democracy movements in Taiwan and South Korea; and the successful campaigns in East Timor and Indonesia.

In the Middle East, we note that the Palestinian struggle to end Israeli apartheid has been by and large nonviolent, from the first Intifada to Gaza's resistance. Many of its key leaders, and nearly a third of Palestinian men, have been jailed. Though the chance for success seems remote, many determined Israeli and Palestinian individuals and grassroots groups work tirelessly for justice and peace. Lebanon, Iran, and even Iraq have their own organized nonviolent movements. In 2011 nonviolent revolutions in Tunisia and Egypt inspired a new wave of nonviolent movements throughout the Arab world.

Africa, too, has a legacy of nonviolence, particularly South Africa's magnificent effort to end apartheid, create democracy, and institutionalize truth and reconciliation. Nonviolent campaigns overthrew the dictator of Madagascar in 1991 and the murderous regime of Charles Taylor in Liberia. Europe and the former Soviet bloc have held massive nonviolent movements from Spain and Portugal to Northern Ireland and Poland. Lech Walesa's Solidarity movement in the 1980s brought democracy to Poland but inspired many other nations and movements, from Czechoslovakia to Estonia.

In East Germany, which was seemingly impervious to revolution, change began in prayer meetings and discussion groups in Leipzig. As these meetings spread, peace marches were held during the 1980s. With the Soviet president Gorbachev's call for *perestroika*, the movements grew exponentially. On October 31, 1989, one East German march drew 300,000 people. A few weeks later, on November 9, 1989, the unthinkable happened. The Berlin wall fell; the stone was moved. Literally. Jubilantly but peacefully. Not a single shot was fired. People walked out of the tomb, across the threshold, into one another's divided nation, entered new life, and embraced.

In another jubilant moment, some three million people joined hands across 430 miles over three Baltic states: Estonia, Latvia, and Lithuania. It was on August 23, 1989, the fiftieth anniversary of the Soviet occupation of the Baltic regions.

In Latin America, grassroots movements brought dictatorships to an end in Chile, Argentina, Bolivia, Venezuela, Brazil, and Uruguay. While poverty, corruption, and violence remain, there have been many tangible victories of justice, democracy, and peace. Costa Rica, in particular, set the standard by abolishing its army and using military funds instead for education, health care, and employment. While war spread throughout Central America, Costa Rica maintained a peaceful civil society.

In the United States, the movements for disarmament, justice, and peace continue, though widely ignored by the media. Millions resisted George W. Bush's wars on Iraq and Afghanistan. On February 12, 2003, over fourteen million people in over 240 cities on every continent demonstrated against the impending U.S. war on Iraq. The largest single peaceful demonstration in the history of the world. The war went on. But February 12 opened our eyes to the strength of ordinary people. As the *New York Times* conceded the next day, there are now two global powers—the American empire and the global grassroots movement for peace.

Today, grassroots movements carry on in nearly every corner of the planet. If they persist in rolling away the stone, they will one day bear the good fruit of justice, peace, and new life. Eventually, if people hear the commandment, take it to heart, and maintain the struggle, the stone will be rolled away before every culture of death and people will walk toward resurrection and life.

Many shake their heads. Nonviolence, they say, can't possibly work. Before some powers, change isn't possible. What difference can anyone make? It's an attitude that betrays a lack of hope for humanity. But on reading the history of the grassroots movements, one finds quite the opposite. The Vietnam War ended, apartheid ended, communism ended, the Berlin Wall fell, the Soviet Union collapsed, and dictatorships have scurried into exile. There is hope. The stone can be rolled away. Even in the United States. Some day America's marmoreal arrogance will soften and its militarism lose steam, and the untold billions of dollars committed to bases around the world and nuclear weapons always on alert will be dispersed instead to the needs of the planet and to the education of every child on the art of nonviolent conflict resolution and peaceful coexistence. Nonviolent change is possible.

We live in the most exciting, hopeful era imaginable because we will be the people who will lead humanity away from the brink into a new world of nonviolence—this was the message of Martin Luther King Jr. speaking before a crowd in Memphis the night before he was assassinated. We can change the world; we can, with our friends, put our shoulder to the stone and see it roll. Join the movement, Dr. King said. Be part of this salvific work. Do what you can to let light into the tomb.

Do we want the stone rolled away?

Jesus stands in the midst of our culture of violence, looks us in the eye, and issues a challenge. He is peaceful, centered, nonviolent, and determined. He wants the stone taken away. *Now.*

Chapter 8

"BY NOW THERE WILL BE A STENCH!": RESISTING THE NONVIOLENT JESUS

Standing before Lazarus's tomb, Jesus commands, "Take away the stone." And how does the great disciple Martha respond? She tries to stop him! Earlier she said, "Yes, Lord. . . . " Now she says, "No, Lord." In effect: "Nothing can be done; Lazarus is gone. You're too late. Face it, death has won."

Here at the height of the story, Jesus' friend and disciple resists the great commandment. "Let the stone remain where it is. Don't trouble us any more—even if you are the Son of God. Even the Son of God must admit the reality of death. Leave us to our misery and despair. Don't disturb my brother's bones. We're having a hard enough time as it is. Please don't make a scene. Please don't make us do something. Please don't disrupt the tomb. We don't want your intervention. We've made peace with death."

And then her last-ditch effort to impress on him the finality of it all: "Lord, by now there will be a stench!"

One of the most comical lines in the Gospel—if it were not so tragic.

There's a parallel here to the Gospel of Luke. In Luke, Peter affirms Jesus as the Messiah, but objects to the idea of Jesus facing torture and execution. Here in John, Martha issues a similar objection. Likewise she objects to his confronting death.

Her objection helps us understand our own predicament. "Lord, by now there will be a stench," she says to Jesus. "He's been dead for four days." It's the voice of raw despair, the voice of no-hope-whatsoever, the voice that says, "Life is a dead end. Once you're dead, you're dead. Evil powers always get the upper hand." Don't we harbor this attitude of disappointment all the time? This is our underlying confession to Jesus: "You're too late. You're absent, irrelevant, impotent. Nothing can be done. Don't bother making us try."

On top of this is the bitter irony. In her objection, Martha tries to prevent Jesus from raising Lazarus! She does what we all do: object to, resist, and disobey the commandment to take away the stone. She knows that exposing the body will be a messy, unseemly affair. She has in mind the scene to follow—the putrid flesh, the swarm of flies, the crusted membranes. And the stench. The Mosaic cleanliness laws will be shot to hell. The month of mourning will be knocked off course. She strives to keep things under control—Jesus included. In the face of death, she tries to manage and control the God of life.

Why would she do this? Why do we? The answer is simple, and shocking: *we do not want resurrection!* The idea of new life sets us on our heels. We can't handle that much hope, that much freedom. The implications overwhelm us. We prefer the comfortable predictability of the culture of death. War is familiar, so long as it doesn't come to our own front door. Predictable too are the Pentagon and the nuclear labs of Los Alamos and the chicanery of Wall Street and the overweening power of transnational corporations. We've made our peace with all the metaphors of death—poverty, capital punishment, unmanned drones, nuclear weapons, and global warming. Trying to keep it distant, we've made peace with the tomb.

Anyone involved in peace-and-justice work knows this first hand: the minute you publicly raise discomfiting questions, you inevitably make a stink. People get upset. They say, "Why are you doing this? Why mess everything up? Everything was fine the way it was. Stop rocking the boat. Stop disturbing our peace! Think of the stench!"

But the commandment comes down, and it won't go away: *take away the stone!*

It's hard to understand why we resist the peacemaking ways of Jesus. But for anyone who cares about the spiritual life, the human family and the fate of the earth, understanding is crucial.

In my own work as a spiritual director, I have seen over and over again how God comes intimately close to love and guide us, and in each instance we pull back. We resist the movement of God. It's a typical human reaction. We fail to recognize God's life-giving work among us as a gift, and we find it hard to recognize our own resistance. This is why a spiritual director is such a treasure. He or she can point out the presence of God in our lives, how God tries to lead us to new life, and how new life is good for us, even our most fundamental desire.

A director challenges us to enter our prayer mindful that God is gentle, loving, and nonviolent; that God wants only what is good for us; that God is trustworthy. God tries to lead us to the fullness of life, to resurrection—and not only individually but as a culture. God wants us to walk out of the tombs of death where we are stuck and unaware. The spiritual life is a long journey of learning not to resist God. As we let go of resistance, hurts, and fear, as we allow God's word to take root in us, we'll find ourselves consoled. We'll become peaceful, even joyful. We will move closer toward oneness with God and creation. We'll feel more alive—and get to work rolling away the stone that others too may walk toward new life.

St. Ignatius, one of the great spiritual teachers of all time, taught that we're not supposed to live in desolation. We are supposed to live in the consolation of God's love and peace—personally, communally, and globally. We're supposed to live life to the full, and to help one another do the same. When we learn not to resist God, and to do what God wants, we discover deeper sources of life. To return to the metaphor, we find ourselves raised to new life. We find ourselves walking out of our own tombs.

This is, after all, John's thesis: God offers us new life. "Take away the stone." The commandment is not rescinded. Move the stone that keeps us under the thumb of death, that imprisons our families and friends in the conventions of death, that deceives our churches into sanctioning war, that makes us all cogs in the nation's killing machine. "Take away the stone." It's a commandment we resist, each one of us. And a commandment we resist corporately too: churches, nations, the entire human family.

And so most of us pass our days as if we are treading water. We barely make it through the array of crises and hardships—family divisions, health issues, job loss, financial difficulties, and tensions and anxieties of all kinds. Little energy remains to acknowledge the realities of war, starvation, executions, nuclear weapons, and climate change. We turn away, preoccupied with surviving our loneliness, despair, and dread. This is how we make peace with death. We find a precarious stasis point at which we hold despair at bay, and we hang on as best we can. In the meantime we grant death leave to stalk the earth and do its worse. So long as we don't have to see its victims. And when that strategy fails finally, in our dark despair we eye our own death as a way out. We know nothing of new beginnings.

Indeed, we live in the stench of death and do not even know it. The nonviolent Jesus would lead us into the fresh air of life and peace.

Seemingly secure at our stasis point, we do not want authentic change. We fear the disruption of our lives. We delude ourselves that this is happiness, though a little introspection will reveal just how exhausted and miserable we are. In fact, keeping awareness at arm's length has exhausted nearly everyone we know. It's our common lot, accommodating the culture of war. "Taking away the stone," we fear, will only make our lives worse, will set us at odds.

Certainly, the media and the government emphasize the point. They tell us it's not in our best interest to look skeptically at the ways of death. Or even to ponder them. Of course it's not in *their* interest that we do. Those who run the culture enjoy their power and privilege. It's in their interest to keep things under control. Large shifts in priorities threaten their lofty perch and, at the first breeze of change, they roll out the propaganda machine that indoctrinates and programs us.

Put shortly: "The way things are is the way things should be."

Movements for justice that raise the cry "Take away the stone" are derided and ignored. Rulers certainly do not want to see the Pentagon disarmed or to see Los Alamos and Livermore Labs converted to peaceful purposes. It would drain the elite of their power of coercion and their capacity to amass wealth. Weapons, they insist, are our true benefactors. Our science of war is our true security.

So our culture has its roots in fear and death. And we who are misled go along complacently with the accelerating cycle downward toward violence. For a culture rooted in death—a culture that spawns wealth from death—must find an outlet for inflicting it.

In our blindness, we think (when we think at all), "It is what it is." The phrase has an almost philosophical ring. But what lies beneath it is a lack of imagination. We cannot imagine any other way. How is a culture free of nuclear weapons possible? Isn't corporate greed just part of the fabric of life? What would a world free from deathly powers even look like? How would a society make such enormous changes in any case? A culture not reliant on armaments? Think of how messy that would be. That fresh air, we presume, would be the worst stench.

Better to keep ideas like that on the fringes and to paint people who espouse such ideas as unbalanced fanatics, unwashed subversives, or ungrateful traitors.

So we squander the promise of John's Gospel, that if we confront death we'll be given new life—a kind of resurrection of family, friends, and community. And then it will dawn on us just how stuck in the stench of despair we were. Only then will we understand that what we regarded as peace and happiness was a phony sham. It was merely a case of playing it safe, of complying with death in the hope that it would pass on by. It's a craven inclination that has all but killed us spiritually.

Martha protests: *Don't make us do that, Jesus!* She tries to stop him. But he's not dissuaded. He turns and puts the question to her: "Did I not tell you that if you believe you will see the glory of God?" We do not remember him ever telling her this. But we know he asked if she believed that he was the resurrection and the life. He had earlier told his disciples that Lazarus's death would reveal the glory of God. Martha, stunned into silence, says no more. His authority prevails. And so we come to the astonishing declaration of verse 41:

They took away the stone.

"Did I not tell you that if you believe you will see the glory of God?" It's a question Jesus puts to each of us. John's Gospel brims with talk about faith and belief, blindness and seeing. It refers many times to Jesus' coming glory and the glory of God. He has come into the world that we might believe, that we might experience the glory of God, and thereby have life to the full.

Martha remains silent. And perhaps that's the best way for us to respond too. Stay with the question in silence; let it linger in the heart. Then get to work rolling away the stone wherever people are mired in the culture of death. If we take on the task and roll away the stone, like Martha, we too will see the glory of God.

Chapter 9

JESUS' PRAYER OF GRATITUDE

At last the stone gets rolled away. Who did it? Not Jesus. He ordered that it be taken away, but the ones who pressed against it and started it rolling were the people themselves. Jesus was the one with the vision, and the people did the work. They started it moving; they got his movement moving. His was the vision and the promise of new life. And when all resisted, he persisted. They did what he said finally because he was adamant. He believed purely, so they believed and obeyed the commandment. His was a staunch and unqualified and novel trust, and it removed the stone from their hearts.

So the stone is taken away, and at this climactic moment, for the first time in all eleven chapters of John's Gospel, Jesus prays. Since we have never seen or heard him pray before in this Gospel, we might be surprised. We might have expected a lecture about the meaning of what just happened or another commandment. Instead, Jesus lifts his eyes and addresses God.

But note: he does not pray according to Martha's instructions, which went along the hackneyed lines of: "God will give you whatever you ask of him." Imagine Martha trying to teach Jesus how to pray! When he does not pray but approaches the tomb and demands action, she resists. Her imagination and understanding falter before Jesus' incomprehensible hope. It was he finally who had a lesson to teach. Jesus, it turns out, is the true spiritual master. It's just that his ways are not ours. At least not yet.

At this moment, with the stone off to the side and the tomb wide open, Jesus speaks directly to God—still not according to what we presume to be Martha's fondest hopes. He doesn't pray, for instance, "God, please take care of Lazarus. Please make Lazarus come alive." In fact, he requests nothing at all. In the Sermon on the Mount, he instructs the disciples not to babble on in prayer like the Pharisees, for "God knows everything that you need." Later, in his discourse, he will announce that anyone who loves him and obeys his commandment can ask for whatever they want in his name and will receive it. But here, he offers the most radical prayer of all. He simply says, "Thank you."

There at the heart of the culture of death, Jesus gives thanks to God that the stone that has us entombed has been moved. This is the prayer of Jesus:

Father, thank you for hearing me. I know that you always hear me but because of the crowd here, I have said this, that they may believe that you sent me.

He addresses God as if to a loving parent with whom he lives in close, intimate relationship. He knows that his loving God listens to him, and loves him, and he is filled with gratitude that God accompanies him on his mission to liberate humanity from the culture of death.

There is in all this an unspoken endorsement of contemplative prayer. If we ever hope to resist death as Jesus modeled, contemplative prayer must become our practice. Only then can we live in relationship to God and revel in gratitude for the sheer gift of life. Only then can we understand and appreciate nonviolent resistance to the culture's deathly ways. Contemplative prayer unleashes our gratitude and celebration for every nonviolent act and movement. Our hearts join with God's in contemplative prayer, and God's desires become our own. Because God's heart lingers over the suffering of the world, our hearts linger there too. With every movement toward life, gratitude springs up from within.

But contemplative prayer takes us further than mere sympathy. God shows us a way to move. And when we do, we gain confidence and come to trust more and more in the surprising ways of the God of life. The ways of violence spiral downward; the spiral of nonviolence ascends against gravity's pull and creatively forges a liberating way up from the grave to new life and resurrection.

If we measure our own prayer against the prayer of Jesus, we discover how unlike him we are. Most of us pray like Martha, hectoring God about outcomes we desire. Behind this impulse of ours is a hidden desire to see God as an entity we can manipulate and control. We bargain. We negotiate. We expect a little reciprocity. (My friend folksinger Dar Williams jokes in one song about how we expect God to do our will—"that's what we pay him for.") But when God lays at our feet the path toward liberation from deathly ways, we object and resist. We cling to mere religion; we want to stay in charge.

Jesus, on the other hand, lives in an intimate relationship with his abiding God, the one who called him "my beloved." Jesus wants God to control *him*, to be in charge of *his* life. And from his lips flows gratitude—gratitude for God's loving care, for God's abiding presence and protection, gratitude mostly that God so loves the world that he would lead humanity from death into resurrection. The two are that united: God's desires are Jesus' desires. And that unity—God with the Son, the Son with the disciples—is the hope of the world. Jesus has in mind that we all follow his example and get swept up in God's love for the world, that we too overflow with new life, resurrection, peace, and gratitude.

The crowd now has heaved the stone from the tomb, and Jesus offers public thanks to God. And we come to understand that the two actions are one and the same. To cling gratefully to God is to join God's campaign for new life. And the aphorism seems just as true the other way around. Campaigners for life incline towards gratitude and hope.

Do the two merge in us, or do we divorce them? We can tell by our visceral response to news about this or that nonviolent action or this or that campaign that goes against the cultural grain. Granted, the media paints participants in unflattering shades. But if we're attuned with God, we'll be thankful for every nonviolent movement against the culture of death—its wars, injustices, double standards, policies of aggression, and stockpiles of arms. We celebrate the victories over death that preceded us; we celebrate the victories to come.

Perhaps our prayer of thanksgiving could go something like this:

> *God of life, thank you for the abolition of slavery, for all those who worked to take away the stone from the culture of slavery, for all those who welcome a new culture of human rights and freedom.*

> *God of life, thank you for the abolition of sexism, for all those who worked to take away the stone from the culture of sexism and violence against women, for all those who welcome a new culture of equality and women's rights.*

> *God of life, thank you for the civil rights movement, for Dr. King and all those who took away the stone of segregation and racism and opened the way for greater racial equality, freedom, and dignity.*

God of life, thank you for the nonviolent movement to abolish apartheid in South Africa, for the leadership of Nelson Mandela and Desmond Tutu, for all those who suffered and gave their lives to take away the stone that entombed black people, for the global movement that helped give birth to a new South Africa and greater justice, truth ,and reconciliation.

God of life, thank you for the peace movement, for those peacemakers who speak out and oppose the world's wars, for those who envision and enact nonviolent ways to resolve international conflict, for an end to the world wars, the Southeast Asian, African, and Central American wars, for those who beat swords into plowshares and help us to spend our resources instead on food, homes, jobs, health care, for those who work for the abolition of nuclear weapons, for those who help turn our cultures of war and violence into cultures of peace and nonviolence.

God of life, thank you for those who organize and lead nonviolent movements for new democracy, for the nonviolent fall of the Berlin Wall and an end to communist dictatorship, for the nonviolent revolutions that bring new freedom to your people.

God of life, thank you for the environmental movement, for those who speak out on behalf of creation, who defend the oceans, mountains, land, sky, and creatures, who resist our environmental destruction, who help us turn from our addiction to fossil fuels to reverse catastrophic climate change and live in harmony and respect with the earth and its creatures.

God of life, thank you for hearing us.

If we are grateful for the modest, loving efforts to enhance justice and peace, God's desire for everyone's fullness of life will gradually take root in our hearts. We will come to believe in Jesus, not only, as the theologians say, as the incarnation of God, but as the Way, the Truth, and the Life. We come to believe in his Way, nonviolent resistance to the culture of death. We come to believe in his Truth: the power to expose the illusions and lies of our cultural proclivity toward violence and war. We come to believe in his Life—his promise that, indeed, all are meant to thrive in peace, hope, and *agape*. Like him, our love for others and gratitude to God will lead us to give our lives for the liberation of everyone, that all might know the fullness of life and resurrection.

This is the challenge he places in our hands. Find a way to join some grassroots movement for disarmament and justice and offer thanks whenever you hear of people hauling away the stone from the tomb. You'll soon realize that Jesus was right. Not only is his Sermon on the Mount method of nonviolent resistance God's will—but it works. As hope begins to blossom within you, you'll increasingly believe in the promise of fullness of life for all, and you'll increasingly find new energy to further oppose the culture's surfeit of death.

It's written in the fabric of our lives. As we believe more and more in Jesus, we will enter into his prayer and let our hopes for new life soar. As we join with the billions around the world who take away the stone from the tomb of injustice, war, and death, we will give thanks and do what we can to keep the movement of nonviolence moving.

The struggle to liberate humanity from the culture of death leads us to a surprising act. Like Jesus, we too will lift our eyes to heaven and whisper in a new language of hope, love, and joy: *thank you, thank you, thank you!*

Chapter 10

THE SECOND COMMANDMENT: "LAZARUS, COME FORTH!"

His gratitude expressed, Jesus issues a second commandment—this time to Lazarus: *Lazarus, come forth!* Our premise all along has been this: Lazarus represents humanity. All of us are dead of spirit, entombed in a culture whose means and purpose and "glory" is death—whether defined as military superiority or racial purity or economic independence or cultural hegemony or national imperialism. All these rely on techniques of threat and coercion and, when push comes to shove, the unleashing of hell. We are all of us entombed in a culture of death. But now Jesus calls out: "Leave your tombs. You are no longer slaves to the culture of war and greed. Live free from the forces of violence and death. I am raising you to fullness of life. No more reliance on the ways of death. I offer you fullness of life."

Here is the climactic moment in the life of Jesus. Here he fulfills his mission to offer life to one and all. He has come perfectly nonviolent, unconditionally loving, infinitely compassionate, and steadfastly truthful. And now his cry: "Come forth." With that begins a nonviolent revolution that continues to this day. And it marks the first day of the rest of our lives.

But one can't help but wonder about poor Lazarus. Time for him has stopped. His lifeless body lies on a slab in the dark.

Inexplicably, the tomb fills with the rumble of grating and groans of exertion and then, dispelling the darkness, rays from the sun. Finally a voice calls his name. Lazarus knows that voice and understands the commandment: "Lazarus, come forth!" His friend, the One who loves him unconditionally, is calling, and the call raises him to life. He hears, rises, and obeys. He appears at the mouth of the cave.

Lazarus, come forth! The word and the work of God. It is the word that summons us to nonviolence and peace, to dignity and simplicity and justice. It beckons us out of addiction and despair into freedom and hope. God's word is always for our betterment. It leads us to healing, love, and peace. In every case it raises us out of our darkest depths into the light of a new day.

Likewise, Jesus' commandment reveals the work of God. Our Higher Power bears the only force that can liberate us from our violence and from complicity with institutions that destroy the weak and devastate the planet. In the beginning, God breathed life. The divine work continues still. Through the nonviolent Jesus, God offers us life by calling us out of death.

We see God's work in those freed from addictions who now celebrate their improbable sobriety and peace. We see it among those who, having surveyed the world's cruelty, sank into depression and despair but who now are on the uplifting journey of promoting peace. We see it in nonviolent movements that work toward democracy, freedom, justice, and peace.

Of the latter, I offer two examples of entombed people who obeyed, as it were, the commandment: "Lazarus, come forth!"

The Singing Revolution in Estonia

In 1939, the Soviet Union invaded the tiny nation of Estonia in an effort to expand its empire. Two years later, the Third Reich on the rise, Germany looked eastward, followed suit, and then purged the land of those who had staffed the Soviet bureaucracies. Three years later the Soviets returned in force and executed a purge of their own. Soldiers shot bullets into the condemned, and the executed crumpled into anonymous communal graves. Battered from east and west, the Estonians bore a terrible weight of fear and grief. All told, many thousands died; seventy thousand fled—this in a tiny nation of less than a million. The land became a tomb.

For decades afterwards, the survivors struggled just to survive. Their identity was in tatters. The Soviets systematically dismantled Estonian culture and erased its history. The hammer and cycle flag was raised, the Estonian flag outlawed.

But the people retained one characteristic unique to Estonia—their love of song. Yearly they gathered at the song festival known as "Laulupidu," held in a massive amphitheater, and sang the traditional songs. Some thirty thousand attended each year, and as the thousands of voices rose, ancient memories and sentiments resurged.

Here was a force the Soviets couldn't conquer. So they tried co-opting it, drafting a repertoire of approved songs—most in praise of Soviet might. But in 1947, a song slipped past Soviet censors, a song with ancient resonances proclaiming the beauty of the Estonian countryside. Every year thereafter the people slogged through the official program, eagerly awaiting the end of the evening when they could sing of their own former glories. The song filled hearts and inspired tears. It had become Estonia's unofficial national anthem.

In 1969, with the centennial of the song festival approaching, the Soviets banned the people's beloved song. Too risky to be sung on such a momentous day. The festival went on, the Soviet functionaries sitting at their place of honor. The authorized program plodded along, and at the conclusion, the maestro exited the stage, the evening all but ended. But then, in fits and starts, unlawful strains took to the air. Voices converged and the competing keys found a center. The prohibited song had been raised, "Land That I Love."

They kept at it, thousands singing spontaneously, until at last the maestro strode back to the stage and, in an act of defiance, conducted it officially, his spine a bit straighter, a smile of pride on his face. As I watched the scene in the documentary *The Singing Revolution*, it dawned on me: here was a sacramental moment, the moment the empire fell. Together, they were responding to the commandment, "Lazarus, come forth."

With defiance now in the air, organizers began working clandestinely, behind the scenes, and in 1987 they grew bold enough to call for a rally. Word spread through the grapevine and to everyone's surprise, thousands showed up. Bravely, people spoke out, putting to the test Gorbachev's new policy of *perestroika* ("relative freedom") and *glasnost* ("free speech").

Later that year, at a planned summer concert, two hundred thousand came. And by now distinctions were blurring between songfest and political rally. Free speech, to the Estonians, means freedom to sing. And singing unleashes yearning for independence. The people joined hands and, each day for a week, sang of hope and pride. Emboldened, a motorcyclist roared by the edge of the crowd and unfurled the Estonian flag. It was an illegal act to display the flag, and it evoked a long raucous cheer.

As the winds of independence picked up, so did the opposition. In occupied Estonia lived thousands of Russians. And just before the occupation came undone, the Russians took countermeasures. They organized a pro-Soviet rally and stormed the government building. Inside, the illegally formed Estonian Congress had taken refuge. Now they were trapped, the mob outside in an agitated mood. Word made its way around, and thousands of

Estonians converged on the scene and surrounded the building. Now it was the Russians who found themselves trapped.

Here was another sacramental moment. No violence erupted or shouts or threats. Rather the people broke into song. Hymns and anthems rose on the air. And after a space of time, the crowd parted and made an aisle. This was no bloody "running the gauntlet"—the Estonians hurt not a soul. The Russians passed through receiving only the harmonies of the people's resolve. Such magnanimity stirs the blood.

The next festival drew some three hundred thousand, one out of every three Estonians. "It was an ocean of people," one said, "waving back and forth." As for the Soviets, they stood by paralyzed. How to justify tear-gassing people for singing?

By now, upheavals plagued much of the Soviet Union. Unrest erupted in Latvia, Lithuania, and Russia. And with every crack in the Soviet system the Estonians creatively filled the void. Tanks rolled in eventually, their first destination: the Estonian television tower. The Soviet empire wanted control of the news.

Again, out surged the people, and around the tower they formed a human shield. Another stand-off, another tense moment. As the people held their ground, soldiers milled about awaiting directions from on high. And then word came down. Russia had seceded from the union—the USSR had finally unraveled. The tanks rolled out of town. Estonia was free. And the people broke out in song. They heard the commandment and emerged from the tomb.

The Women's Revolution in Liberia

The second tale comes from the West African nation of Liberia, where in 2003, ordinary, unarmed women by the thousands heard the command of Jesus and launched a campaign of steadfast nonviolent resistance that ended a civil war, disarmed the rebels, and swept a dictator from power. In the process they laid the groundwork for a new democracy and saw to the election of Liberia's first woman president. The only resource they had—the power of nonviolence. Together they rolled away the stone, called their people forth, and let them live in peace.

Liberia is a country of three million. Freed slaves from America founded it in 1847. But for more than a century, their descendents dominated the nation brutally. The people suffered under poverty and repression until, in 1989, civil war erupted. Matters grew worse; years of terror followed: torture, rape, starvation, and murder. By 2002, more than twenty thousand had died; one in three were driven from their homes.

Then the women of Liberia rose up. And a leader emerged: Leynab Gbowee, courageous and articulate. Together the women declared themselves sick of war, sick of rape, sick of starving. They wanted peace. And, against conventional wisdom, they worked for it nonviolently.

The terror centered on Charles Taylor, at once a churchgoing Christian and a brutal tyrant. He came to power in 1996—a man, they say, who could offer you a warm smile and then order your execution. One night he might lead a prayer service; the next day he would order the massacre of his opponents. He conscripted battalions of young boys and gave them the taste of gratuitous killing. These were his death squads. Hiding behind them, he embezzled enormous sums from the national treasury.

In June 2002, Leynab Gbowee had a dream. In it, she invited the women of Liberia to come to a church and there discuss how they might make peace. She awoke and pondered the matter and set about to make the dream come true. She issued the invitation and hundreds turned out. With them, she founded the Women's Peace Movement. Her call became the voice of Jesus crying out loudly, "Lazarus, come forth."

Originally their name was to be the Christian Women's Initiative. But one woman, Asatu Ban Kenneth, spoke up. She was Muslim and objected to the name. Here was a critical moment: What to do? Leynab quickly settled matters. She proclaimed the movement open to women of all religions and creeds. Women were the nation's only hope, and none would be rejected.

Instinctively, the Christian women objected in return: they had no desire to participate with Muslims. An early impasse for the fledgling group. But Leynab was ready, and she posed a question, a kind of a koan: "Does a bullet know a Christian from a Muslim?" The question pierced deep and swept aside differences. They realized, in their common losses they were one. And overwhelmingly Muslim women were embraced as sisters. The struggle was on.

They started off modestly, doing what they could. They prayed and fasted. Still, the killing went on. Rebels and warlords rampaged in the countryside; Taylor's death squads rampaged in the city. Everyone everywhere was terrorized. And in March 2003, the violence surged. Rebels went on a wide spree of rape, torture, and murder. And thousands fled to Monrovia, the capital, and found asylum of sorts in makeshift refugee camps.

Taylor in turn issued a decree, one without mercy. In the name of Jesus he evicted them back to the countryside—to take their dismal chances there. "Taylor could pray the devil out of hell," one woman said in passing. He was a man of angelic piety and demonic violence, a fearsome mystery.

In April 2003 conditions in the capital began to deteriorate quickly. Forces were converging, threatening total warfare. "We had to do something forceful and fast," Leynab recalled. "So we organized a rally and asked the woman who ran the Catholic radio station to broadcast it."

The organizers weren't sure what to do, so they opened their Bibles and read from Esther, heroine to her own people. The Liberian women were emboldened to do the same and fashioned a modest plan. Why not wear white, symbol of peace, and sit near the fish market, where Taylor often passed in his limousine?

The sit-in was attended by twenty-four hundred women— the first time in their history that Christian and Muslim women had publicly acted together. They sang and chanted: "We are tired of suffering, we are tired of rape, we are tired of war. We want peace." Their banner read: "The women of Liberia want peace now."

It was a gesture that put their lives at risk. They dared contest Liberia's perpetrators of violence. That is, the men. "We knew we were going to get killed," one woman says, "but by taking this action, we thought, at least we will have died for peace."

The women had spoken, and Taylor was enraged. He hotly denounced and ridiculed them. Every now and then he drove by, furious and confounded. They camped out for a week.

As the week passed, the women began to befriend one another and build community; they derived from each other a sense of strength. And they grew creative: What tactics might they employ to press their demands? One tactic they settled on goes back to ancient Greek literature—to Aristophanes. No sexual relations with their husbands until the war ends. As one woman later said, "All our husbands began to pray with us for an end to the war."

But the war continued. Rebels raided the camp and left some dead. Hours later, government troops did the same. The women concluded that the only way to end the war was to get both sides to meet. They went to the Parliament building, sat down, and there demanded that all sides negotiate. Thousands of women came. And the contagion swept the city. More and more came, women marching in droves, waving signs and singing for peace.

Finally shamed, Taylor agreed to a meeting. The occasion marks one of the great nonviolent confrontations in recent history. On April 23, 2003, with five hundred women behind her and lordly Taylor enthroned on a chair on the stage, the heroine Leynab Gbowee presented the women's case.

The speech shone with rhetorical brilliance and it concluded powerfully: "The women of Liberia are tired of war. We are tired of running; we are tired of begging for food, we are tired of our children being raped. We want a future for our children." Taylor listened impassively and then conceded. He would attend peace talks.

Word spread quickly, and all of Africa began talking about Liberia's heroic nonviolent women. Only one other thing was needed: to corral the opposing side.

Two days later a contingent of women headed toward Sierra Leone, where the rebels had their camp. When they arrived they found rebels and warlords in a swanky hotel, coddling themselves like kings. The women in white lined the street and held up their placards. The rebels were taken aback. But the vigiling continued, and the rebels succumbed. They would attend peace talks as well.

A date was set, June 4, 2003; the place, Accra, Ghana. The two factions would meet face to face. The women, however, were incredulous. They knew enough that there would be no progress unless they were there. So they appealed for funds to make the trip.

Money rolled in from all over the nation, enough to fund a delegation of hundreds. When deliberations got underway, the women were there, outside the doors, dressed in white. Quite a scene: inside, murderers and marauders, and on the street, the implacable women demanding peace. "We are your conscience," they said. A vague warning.

The peace talks got underway but then stalled. And the women got frustrated. "What is this, a vacation?" they complained. Their frustration was well founded for, meanwhile, back in Monrovia, order collapsed completely. There was little food and water to be had, and thousands fled for shelter to the city stadium.

The tearful women in Accra redoubled their efforts. "Give us peace now," they sang. Their signs multiplied, proclaiming, "No more guns, no more war." Everyone entering or leaving the building got an earful.

When back in Monrovia a rebel missile struck the U.S. Embassy, where displaced people were harbored, the women surrounded the building in Accra and linked arms. Until the carnage ended, they said, they would not leave.

A mocking security guard announced over the PA system: "The peace talks have been seized by General Leynab and her troops. . . ."

The women had locked them down. And when a warlord appeared at the door, trying to pass by, Leynab ordered: "Go back in there and sit down. If you were a real man, you wouldn't be killing your people. That's why I have to treat you like a boy. Go back and sit down and negotiate peace!"

Slowly, the tide turned. The international community got involved, and on August 11, 2003, Taylor left for Nigeria, setting off days of celebrations. But the women knew their work was not over. A transitional government was put into place, and the women knew they had to monitor its every decision.

Meanwhile they took up the thorny issue of forgiveness. "The men make all the mistakes," Leynab said. "They brought war and poverty." Oceans of blood were on their hands. How to forgive them? They discussed it and tried, reaching out first to ex–child soldiers, seeing in the boys' eyes the boys' own brutal victimization.

Finally, in January 2006 the general elections took place, a day of improbable achievement. Elected president of Liberia that day was Ellen Johnson Sirleaf, the first woman in all of Africa ever elected to such high office. "Icing on the cake," Leynab said with cool nonchalance. Reflecting years later in the powerful documentary film *Pray the Devil Back to Hell*, she said: "We stepped out and did the unimaginable."

Indeed they did. And in doing the unimaginable, they have so much to teach us. About faith and nonviolence, prayer and struggle. About giving our lives for justice and disarmament. About vision and imagination. About strength, power, and fearlessness. About changing the world. In sum, about raising the dead and leading them into their new lives of freedom and peace.

Hearing the Commandment

You and I are Lazarus, and we need to listen for the calling of our names. Attune your ear and hear Jesus address you personally. Take the words to heart, listen really hard, and find the strength to arise from whatever kills the spirit and destroys us as a people. Then you'll approach the One who summons us to new life and be able to help others join what we might call a resurrection movement.

I suggest we say the words aloud—during meditation, during the day, as we awake and before we sleep. "Lazarus, come forth." Hear them as if you yourself are implicated in our nation's violence, mired in its warfare, helpless before its imperial aims.

Notice what parts inside stir to new life. Notice what it feels like
to come alive and cast off your death shroud. Let yourself rise
and approach the liberating voice.

Lazarus, come forth! If we heed the voice, like the Estonians
and the Liberians, we'll see the light of a new day. On that day
we'll receive God's gifts of love, life, and peace. We'll be filled
with consolation and joy. "Free at last," as Dr. King was fond of
saying.

"Lazarus, come forth" are *the* prophetic words of Jesus—the
very voice of God. "Humanity, come forth!" And as we obey we
will find ourselves equipped to share in Jesus' mission of liberation. His ways of nonviolence, compassion, and peace will
become ours. His prophetic words will be on our lips.

We can do this. The Gospel writer has given us the key to
understanding. We can, like Jesus, approach the epicenter of
the culture of death and declare audaciously: "Humanity, come
forth!" And as we see once benighted people enter the light of
peace, Jesus' consolation and gratitude will be our own.

Then all humanity will join with Dr. King: "Free at last, free at
least, thank God Almighty, we're free at last."

Chapter 11

THE THIRD COMMANDMENT: "UNBIND HIM AND LET HIM GO FREE!"

Lazarus appears, but bound in burial clothes. We are told in vivid detail: he was "tied hand and foot with burial bands, and his face was wrapped in a cloth." He can neither hear, see, speak, walk, nor reach out—each a symbolic function of being a disciple of Jesus. He cannot hear or speak the Word of God. He can't see Christ in others or reach out in loving service. He remains trapped, even though he wobbles at the entrance, in the culture of death.

There is therefore one more task at hand. Hence Jesus' issues a third commandment: "Unbind him and let him go free!" He won't leave bewildered Lazarus in the lurch. He sees the project to the end, freeing Lazarus for life to the full. Once again Jesus directs his commandment to the people of Bethany. First he told them to take away the stone, and now to unbind Lazarus. He has them approach the formerly dead man and put their trembling hands on the burial wraps and then to clean him up and set him free. They must, in brief, embrace him, offer compassion, and welcome him back. If they had truly mourned him, they would rejoice to undertake this work of mercy.

How well do they respond? We don't know. On that matter, the Gospel is silent. We've come to the end of the story: the once dead man stands at the mouth of the tomb awaiting the people to unbind him.

One thinks the crowd's eyes grew big as silver dollars. Before them stands a dead man in a death shroud. They cast their looks between the two—first at Lazarus and then at Jesus, who had just said to unbind him. *Touch him? Are you kidding?*

He is, of course, eventually unbound: though it goes unnarrated. We gather this from Lazarus's appearance in the next chapter at a party thrown in Jesus' honor. Lazarus, like Jesus, has become something of a celebrity.

The same image appears in Mark's Gospel, though, under Mark's pen, inversely. Mark's Jesus speaks of "binding the strong man" so that Jesus can plunder the house of the ruler of the world. A strange parable to describe God forcibly invading the world of death.

John's Gospel flips Mark's imagery: Jesus commands that we "unbind the weak and let them go free." For John, this is the work at hand. Everyone in the scene is called upon to join in.

How might we do this? John's Jesus commands us to spend our lives unbinding sisters and brothers bound by our culture of violence. For the rest of our lives, we are to help liberate others, setting them free from uncritical obedience to the culture. This is the work that Jesus assigns to each of us. Liberate everyone! Unbind everyone! Release everyone to live freely and in peace. The challenge hangs in the air.

In a world where global destruction looms, this is an enormous undertaking. The genius of the Gospel is that the story ends there, with Jesus' third commandment neither acted upon nor ignored. The work remains. Each of us needs to turn our attention toward those who are bound—the poor and the homeless, the hungry and the sick, the imprisoned and marginalized, the disabled and the elderly—and even the so-called enemy. Anyone straddling the threshold of death.

To fulfill Jesus' commandment, we need not travel far. In one way or other, we all need to be unbound, beginning with ourselves. After us come our families, friends and neighbors, and beyond, through grassroots movements, the entire human race. No matter our station in life or how we make a living, we are all of us summoned to unbind humanity.

Setting Ourselves Free

All of us stand at the mouth of the tomb, bound in some measure by the culture of violence and war. We may not realize the extent to which we are bound, but as we reach out to others, we need to let them help us as well.

Could Lazarus free himself? No, and neither can we. He was dead, trapped, stuck. Jesus called him forth from the tomb, and somehow Lazarus managed to shuffle out, making his way toward the light and the muffled voice that called him. But he could get no farther. He needed help. So he stood and waited to be unbound.

You and I are very much like him. We must, first of all, participate in our own resurrection. Take the difficult first steps, lurch toward the veiled light, stand at the doorway. Jesus will send people to disentangle our limbs from the cloths and unwind the gauze from our faces. But the first efforts are ours: we must stumble in good faith toward the light.

What is it that keeps us bound? What part of the culture of death impedes our seeing, hearing, speaking, reaching out and walking a path of new life? These are questions worth pondering—life-and-death questions that lie at the heart of the spiritual life.

Half the struggle is to know in the first place that we are bound by the culture. Our greatest need may be to become aware of our entrapment. My friend Patty says that in the United States there are only two kinds of people: those who have had therapy and those who haven't. She says most of us pass our lives oblivious to the weightiness of the childhood and cultural influences that bind us. Jungian analyst Robert Johnson puts it more playfully. There are, he says, three movements of life: at first we are unconsciously conscious and then consciously unconscious. Finally, if we are able, we become consciously conscious.

In any event, the first few breaths are ours to take. And then we need to shake away our grogginess and face our predicament and do our best to stumble out of darkness. Prayer, spirituality, therapy, community, public action, and participating in grassroots movements for disarmament and liberation—all of these can be avenues toward inner freedom and new life.

The twelve step program offers one solution. It acknowledges we all feel pain, and our urge is to try to escape it through addictions—to alcohol, drugs, sex, work, gambling, consumerism. Our addictions lay heavy on us and keep us bound. But through naming our addiction, working with a support group and counselor, turning to our Higher Power, and living mindfully a day at a time, we can discover a new life of sobriety. The twelve steps unbind us and set us free. Indeed, they hold the promise of a new lease on life.

For instance, many are stuck in the rat-race to luxuriate in opulence. Stuck in a cycle of greed, we go relentlessly after money, yet never find satisfaction. Our byword becomes *more*—and more than a byword, an obsession. We cling to our stuff and our status until our dying days. And only then, when our grasping finally strikes us as trivial, do we let go. But Jesus summons us to break free now. Life depends not on satisfying greed. Life springs from freedom, life springs from *agape*.

Morever, since violence has been the backdrop of our lives, it's no surprise that we're addicted to it. It gives us a charge, unites us around the television, instills a false sense of transcendence and omnipotence. It also instills, when woven into our entertainment, a vague sense of fear. In our welter of fear we are inclined to hand over our civil rights in exchange for protection against hyped-up threats. The Patriot Act comes to mind. More than that, fear inclines us to give the government a blank check to put the condemned to death and conduct wars in our name.

Some out of fear stockpile guns in their homes. And even if we don't go that far, there lurks temptations toward racism and sexism, forms of violence in themselves. We are trapped in violence, stuck in the illogicality of *we take lives to save lives*. Violence has come to seem normal, practical, part of God's plan.

But from the perspective of the nonviolent Jesus—the one who said, "If you live by the sword, you'll die by the sword"— violence spirals insidiously toward the hell of death unquestioned and unchallenged. Violence adds nothing to life. The God of life rejects violence, and Jesus, God's ambassador, calls us to reject it too.

But we can't do it alone; we need help. Like Lazarus, like the alcoholic, we need others to unfurl our burial cloths, the layers upon layers keeping us stuck. So thoroughly programmed to violence are we that our journey toward nonviolence will take us the rest of our days.

Saints throughout the ages taught we need a guru, a spiritual guide, a priest or minister or elder or healer or a community to set us free. Such guides present us with vision to see a new way of living. They offer the sense of inner hearing to discern Jesus' call to Gospel peacemaking. They free our voices to prophetically announce God's reign reflected in the way of Jesus. They untie our hands so we can reach out to others in loving service. They set our feet on the road to peace.

I've said it before: most of us have grown comfortable with death. The challenge, then, is to recognize our need and choose the way of life. Freedom and fullness of life are ours for the taking.

Setting Free Those around Us

As we become freer, we need to busy ourselves unbinding those around us, beginning with those closest at hand—our relatives, children, friends, and neighbors. Conscious, compassionate, and nonviolent, we are to clothe our friends in dignity and honor. In so doing we free them and welcome them back to the land of the living.

I have said we fear the ramifications of resurrection. On the other hand, a part of us yearns for this freedom. Just a little consciousness makes us aware; we don't want to be blind, deaf, mute, paralyzed. At the edges of our consciousness we all desire the life of peace and promise that Jesus offers.

How to help others find it? Perhaps volunteer at a local shelter or soup kitchen, at a hospital or a school. Financially support a relief organization. Put in time at a local church or non-profit organization doing good. Wherever people yearn to be free from violence, poverty, and injustice, there's work to do. Each of us is needed. Each can make a difference.

I remember once, for example, speaking passionately to a crowded church in Phoenix on the lessons of nonviolence from Jesus and St. Francis. The room was energized, people were excited, and our closing prayer service sent us forth to be instruments of Christ's peace. Afterwards, a man approached me at the podium and asked, "Are you saying that Jesus and Francis would not want me to keep my arsenal of guns and bullets, that they want me to get rid of them and love and serve others instead?" I looked at him incredulously, for indeed I had spent the entire day saying just that. "Yes, of course," I answered. "Well, then, I promise I will throw all my guns and bullets in a pit and bury them in concrete if you tell me to do so." I told him to do that immediately. The next day he emailed me to say that his weapons were buried, and he felt freer already.

Setting Free Those Most in Need

Our story climaxes with Jesus calling on the bystanders, as it were, to unbind humanity and free one another to cast off violence, poverty, and war. Or put more succinctly, to cast off death in all its forms. This is nothing less than permission to change the world! Structures, systems, institutions: they all must change. Jesus wants no one trapped in the culture of war. "For God so loved the world. . . ." Jesus wants all to live life to the full.

Isn't that what Nelson Mandela and Archbishop Tutu did? And the global movement to abolish apartheid? They unbound black South Africans from the evil of apartheid and led them to a new national freedom. They changed the structures of a nation.

Isn't that what Dr. King and the civil rights movement did? They unbound African Americans from the evils of white supremacy and segregation and led them into a new national freedom. They forced the president's hand. President Johnson signed the Voting Rights Act into law, and the structures of a nation changed.

Isn't that what anti-war movements do, and movements to protect the ecology and movements to end poverty and abolish

nuclear weapons? All of them are busy trying to unbind humanity from all manner of death and liberate the culture toward
nonviolence and peace.

It is ours to free the human race from death in all its guises.
This is the spiritual work that the Gospel demands. Yes, we are
to praise God, say our prayers, and worship. But the God of
life, as revealed by the nonviolent Jesus, did not create humanity to languish in tombs. God's work is unfinished. Our job is to
finish it.

In our story, Jesus commands, "Unbind him." Do they obey
him? We don't know. At the end of our tale, Lazarus still stands
at the mouth of the tomb—awaiting our help.

Our mission couldn't be clearer. We are to unbind humanity
from the shroud of death and set it free to live in peace. It falls to
us to create a new culture of life, nonviolence, and justice. Only
then can all live in peace. This is the task before us.

We have our work cut out for us.

Part III

SERVING THE GOD OF LIFE

Amen, amen, I say to you, unless a grain of wheat falls to the ground and dies, it remains just a grain of wheat; but if it dies, it produces much fruit. Whoever loves his life loses it, and whoever hates his life in this world will preserve it for eternal life. Whoever serves me must follow me, and where I am, there also will my servant be. The Father will honor whoever serves me.

–John 12:24–26

Whoever loves me will keep my word, and my Father will love her, and we will come to her and make our dwelling with her.

–John 14:23

No one has greater love than this, to lay down one's life for one's friends. You are my friends if you do what I command you. This I command you: love one another. –John 15:13–14, 17

My kingdom does not belong to this world. If my kingdom did belong to this world, my attendants would be fighting to keep me from being handed over to the Judeans. But as it is, my kingdom is not here. –John 18:36

Chapter 12

SERVING THE GOD OF LIFE
INSTEAD OF
THE CULTURE OF DEATH

How to serve the God of life, when we as a culture are hell-bent on taking what is not ours, waging war, and risking environmental destruction? The answer is plain and simple—and few buy into it. To serve God and live life fully we must withdraw our cooperation from the forces of death. And more than withdraw. Our task is more proactive, more assertive. And to capture its essence, Gandhi coined a clumsy word. We are to "non-cooperate" with the forces of death. We resist the big business of death and put our energies into those projects that bring greater life to others, especially the poor and starving.

Over the years, my friends and I have experimented with a myriad of creative nonviolent actions to call sisters and brothers out of their tombs into the new life of peace. One attempt took place on Holy Thursday 2009 at three o'clock in the afternoon. Fourteen of us entered the precincts of Creech Air Force Base near Indian Springs, Nevada. There we planned to pray but also to speak out against the Unmanned Aerial Vehicles, known commonly as "drones," which make practice runs at Creech in preparation to rain fire from the sky over Central Asia.

Ours, as we regard it, was a humble effort to approach a tomb, call the soldiers forth and unbind them, and set them free on the path of nonviolence. Alas, as these things often go, we were placed under arrest. First they slapped on the steel handcuffs and then bound us in chains. Then a night in jail in Las Vegas, about an hour away. On Good Friday morning, they set us free and following the example of the apostles in Acts, we returned to the scene of the crime. There, on the edges of the base, we prayed and said our piece about our national obsession with warmaking.

It's beautiful in the Nevada desert: yucca plants, Joshua trees, the barren sandy landscape, and in the distance snowy mountains. Driving into Indian Springs is a meditation in itself. Our nonviolent action, too, was beautiful. Praying and singing, our group clutched white roses in honor of the White Rose movement in Germany, the small band of students who were executed for leafleting and speaking out against the Nazis.

Quite possibly ours was the first protest at Creech, certainly its first occasion of civil disobedience. In our hands were signs calling for an end to the drones and an appeal to the base commander. We brought along bread and water, too—gifts to the soldiers. Behind a series of brown buildings, a black drone took to the sky and circled over a distant mountain, practicing for the kill.

The first to notice our approach was a young airman on watch, his eyes on high alert, a weapon slung over his shoulder. He reached for it and swung it toward us. His order notwithstanding, we moved ahead and began to sing. He came undone at our dismissing his orders, and he resorted to shoving us with his machine gun. One friend absorbed the first shove, and I took the next.

By now his alarm had turned to fury, so we took to our knees. Three others approached, all armed to the teeth. Together they barked and shouted as if that would make a difference. As for us, we assured them we were unarmed and offered them our roses. The poor airmen—paralyzed and befuddled. What to do? Shout louder? Open fire? Whatever their standard operation procedure, it failed them in the face of nonviolence. In the meantime another drone buzzed overhead.

And so there we were, at something of an impasse. We sat and knelt for hours, the baffled airmen keeping watch, grimacing, pacing. Eventually the Nevada highway patrol arrived, chained us together, and hauled us away.

Said the police sergeant casually: Had we gone on a few steps farther, the airmen would have opened fire. Kathy Kelly of Voices for Creative Nonviolence offered him a rose and posed the question: "Do you think that would have been a crime?"

"No," returned the sergeant, smiling, "they're authorized to shoot."

"Would it have been a shame?" she pressed him.

"Yes," he admitted glumly, "it would have been a shame."

Most were hauled away in police cars and driven the hour to Las Vegas. The last to go, my friends Jerry Zawada and Brian Terrell and I, waited an hour more for a police van to arrive. We sat on the ground in our chains, police officers flanking us as the sky slipped into pink, then, with the setting of the sun, into orange.

Our transportation arrived finally, a filthy van outfitted with metal benches and down the aisle a metal wall. They squeezed the three of us along one side, chained and buckled in. And off to Vegas we went.

Along the way we prayed aloud—for our friends and supporters; for an end to the drones and U.S. wars; for the people of

Iraq, Afghanistan, and Pakistan; for the church's conversion to Holy Thursday nonviolence. We recalled the words of the risen Jesus to the disciple Peter, "When you were younger you went about and did what you wanted, but as you grow older, someone will place a belt around you and take you where you'd rather not go. Follow me." We looked at each other knowingly.

Night by now had fallen, and we drove toward the towering lights of Las Vegas. The streets were mobbed; the scene was dazzling. But mesh on the windows kept us from getting a clear view, an appropriate perspective for the Christian in such a culture. As I joked before church audiences later, it was a good way to see the Strip. Eventually we arrived at the Clark County Detention Facility.

Welcome to the belly of Sin City.

For the next five hours, we languished in a large room with the hundreds of others arrested that night on the streets of Las Vegas. One by one we were fingerprinted, photographed, and booked. Our property was taken and documented. A nurse examined us and took our blood pressure. (Mine was very high, but then, "You're under a lot of stress," she said. She had no idea.)

Around midnight, guards split us up. The men got shuttled off to a concrete cell, and the women to a cell down the hall. There we remained until morning on Good Friday, when we were escorted to the streets, now barren and empty, the revelers in bed nursing hangovers and bemoaning their losses.

It was a difficult night but bearable because of the prayer, our intent, and the sustaining friendships. I felt blessed to be with many close friends and heroes, like Jerry and Brian, but also Steve Kelly, Louie Vitale, and Kathy Kelly. We took the time to catch up on each other's lives and share the highlights of our work. We kept an eye on each other and tried to lift each other's spirits.

The ordeal, while grim, also carried a spirit of playfulness and antics. The women, wisely, fell asleep right away on the concrete floor—after Kathy cheered them up with a rousing song and dance routine. But they accused us, the men, of carrying on a party. Our talking and laughing drifted their way all night long. It began with Steve, maestro of silly jokes, who had us doubled over in laughter. We settled down after a bit and shared our stories and buoyed one another's spirits after a nerve-wracking day. There in our dungeon, we were filled with a sense of irrepressible life.

On a more solemn note, I regard our modest gesture as an act of prayer. As I marched into the maw of the beast, I was mindful of the millions across the country kneeling in pews in gorgeous sanctuaries at Holy Thursday Mass, and the contrast of our sitting in chains in the county jail. Some of us spoke of feeling in solidarity with the nonviolent Jesus, himself arrested on this holy night. We reflected on his last words, "Put down the sword! Stop, no more of this!"—a message we had brought to Creech.

We felt the loneliness of Jesus' arrest, jailing, and trial, yet we felt grateful that we could taste something of his experience. Our nonviolent action, in the end, was a poor but sincere effort to follow Jesus. Our intent was to carry on his campaign of nonviolent resistance to empire and to preach liberation to those stuck in the culture of war. We had gone to the gates of Creech to say: "Take away the stone. Come forth, dead Lazarus. Unbind him, set him free." Successful or not, we felt blessed in the effort.

On Trial for Calling Lazarus Forth

It is strange that when people of faith and conscience—from Jesus to Dr. King—act against the forces of death, the state resorts to death to punish them. This dynamic is a constant throughout history. But the Gospel teaches that we need not fear. We are free to suffer for resistance, perhaps even die at the hands of the state. It's the paschal mystery, old as time: the precarious journey of nonviolent resistance may lead to death, but it leads in the end to new life.

Theologian William Stringfellow explained this dynamic succinctly in November 1968 when he stood before a Baltimore congregation during the trial of nine who, in Catonsville, Maryland—as a gesture of resistance—had burned Vietnam draft files. Stringfellow reminded the people gathered:

> *Remember that the state has only one power it can use against human beings: death. The state can persecute you, prosecute you, imprison you, exile you, and execute you. All of these mean the same thing. The state can consign you to death. The grace of Jesus Christ in this life is that death fails. There is nothing the state can do to you, or to me, which we need fear.*

We need not fear court, prison, persecution, or death. Our task is to seek God, to resist the guises of death, to live life to the full, and to help set every human being free.

A year and a half after our nonviolent action at Creech, the fourteen of us were summoned to stand trial in the Las Vegas County Courthouse. At the start, the judge announced that he would not allow any testimony on international law, the necessity defense, or the drones, only what pertained to the specific charge of "criminal trespassing." With that, the prosecutors called forth a base commander and a local police chief to testify that we had entered the base, that they had given us warnings to leave, and that they arrested us. They testified that they remembered each one of us. Then they rested their case.

We called three expert witnesses, what the newspaper called "some of the biggest names in the modern anti-war movement": Ramsey Clark, former U.S. attorney general under President

Lyndon Johnson; Ann Wright, a retired U.S. Army colonel and one of three former U.S. State Department officials who resigned on the eve of the 2003 invasion of Iraq; and Bill Quigley, legal director for the New York City–based Center for Constitutional Rights. We presumed they would not be allowed to speak. But lo and behold, the judge let them talk, and they testified for hours.

They were brilliant. They spoke about the meaning of "trespassing," and the so-called necessity defense and international law, which allows citizens to break minor laws in adherence to a higher law. Ramsey Clark, looking like Atticus Finch on the stand, said it was a duty.

They cited the classic example of someone driving down a street, seeing a house on fire, noticing a child in the third floor window, hearing the screams, breaking through the front door, violating the no-trespass law, and entering the house to save the child.

"[People] are allowed to trespass if it's for the greater good —and there are certainly exceptions [to the law] when there is an emerging, urgent need," said Quigley. He cited the history of protesters who broke petty laws, from our nation's founders to the Suffragists to the civil rights activists who illegally sat in at lunch counters. In the long run, we honor them for obeying a higher law, for helping to bring us toward justice, he said. Unfortunately, there is a gap between "the law" and "justice," and so, he explained, the struggle today is to narrow that gap. The best test is through "a hundred-year vision," he explained. That is, how will this law and ruling be seen one hundred years from now?

Through carefully crafted questions, the defendants were able to extract several key points from their witnesses:

• Intentional killing is a war crime, as embodied in U.S. constitutional law.

- Drone strikes by U.S. and coalition forces kill a disproportionate number of civilians.

- People have the right, even the duty, to stop war crimes.

- According to the Nuremberg principles, individuals are required to disobey domestic orders that cause crimes against humanity.

After our experts testified, we rested our case. Then Brian Terrell stood up and delivered a short, spontaneous closing statement, one of the most moving speeches I have ever heard. Here are excerpts:

> *Several of our witnesses have employed the classic metaphor when talking of a necessity defense. There's a house on fire, and a child crying from the window and there's a no trespassing sign on the door. Can one ignore the sign, kick down the door and rescue the child? It was a great privilege for us to hear Ramsey Clark, a master of understatement, who put it best. "Letting a baby burn to death because of a no trespass sign would be poor public policy." I submit that the house is on fire and babies are burning in Afghanistan, Iraq, and Pakistan because of the activities at Creech Air Force Base.*

> *The baby is burning also in the persons of the young people who are operating the drones from Creech AFB, who are suffering from post-traumatic stress disorder at rates that even exceed that of their comrades in combat on the ground.*

> *Colonel Ann Wright testified that soldiers do pay attention to what is going on in the public forum, and that they do respond to a "great debate" in the public sphere. There is no great debate going on about drone warfare in our country. Some have noted that the trend toward using drones in warfare is a paradigm shift*

that can be compared to what happened when an atomic bomb was first used to destroy the city of Hiroshima in Japan.

When Hiroshima was bombed, though, the whole world knew that everything had changed. Today everything is changing, but it goes almost without notice. I hesitate to claim credit for it, but there is certainly more discussion of this issue after we were arrested for trespassing at Creech on April 9, 2009, than there was before.

Judge, we appreciate the close attention you've given to the testimony you've heard here. The question that you asked Bill Quigley—"Aren't there better ways of making change than breaking the law?"—is a question we are often asked and that we often ask ourselves.

It was a question that was asked of Rev. Martin Luther King Jr. in 1963 when he was in jail in Birmingham, Alabama. Several clergy people of Birmingham wrote a letter to Dr. King asking him the very same questions that you asked Professor Quigley. Isn't there a better way? Why sit-ins? Why marches? Why protests? Isn't negotiation the better way?

Dr. King's reply to these questions—in his famous Letter from the Birmingham Jail, which is regarded by many as one of the finest things ever written in the English language—heartily agreed that negotiation is the better way. But he said that a society that refuses to face crucial issues needs "nonviolent gadflies" using direct action to raise the level of awareness and raise the level of "creative tension" for a society to rise from the depths of monologue to the majestic heights of dialogue, where the great debate that Colonel Ann Wright says we need, can happen.

The house is on fire. And we fourteen are ones who have seen the smoke from the fire and heard the cries of the children. We cannot be deterred by a No Trespassing sign from going to the burning children.

As he finished, Brian burst into tears and sat down. Many in the courtroom wept. Then the judge stunned us by announcing that he needed three months to "think about all of this" before he could render a verdict. There is more at stake here than the usual meaning of trespassing, he noted. The prosecutors were clearly frustrated and disappointed. With that, he assigned us a court date four months later, thanked us, and said, "Go in peace!" Everyone applauded.

"By all accounts, the Creech 14 trial is the first time in history an American judge has allowed a trial to touch on possible motivations of anti-drone protesters," the local paper said.

Four months later on January 27, 2011, we returned to court. After telling us how "nice" it was to see us, the judge presented each of us with a twenty-page legal ruling explaining why he found us guilty. You argued a defense of necessity, he said, "when an inherent danger is present and immediate action must be taken," such as breaking a no-trespassing law to uphold a higher law and save life. "In this case, no inherent danger was present, and so I find you guilty." In the end he sentenced us to time served. We didn't go to jail, and meanwhile, our drones continued to drop bombs. A new report says unauthorized U.S. drone strikes in 2010 alone claimed nearly twelve hundred lives. According to Pakistani sources, our drone attacks kill almost fifty civilians for every "militant" we target.

Together, through our action and our courtroom testimony, we argued that we could do better than drop bombs through these drone machines. As we left the courtroom, we pledged to continue to speak out against the drones, to try to wake one another up about the U.S. wars in Afghanistan and Pakistan, and to stir the embers of the peace movement to speak out and take action for a new world of nonviolence. We gave thanks for the opportunity to witness to peace, and we went forward determined to promote peace with everyone.

The Church's Mission

In the Gospel of John, Jesus commissions the church to live the fullness of life by fulfilling Jesus' three commandments—Take away the stone! Lazarus, come forth! Unbind him and set him free! How well is the church fulfilling its task?

In history we'll find moments and movements of heroic faithfulness to the Gospel—from the early martyrs to the Franciscans of the Middle Ages. And more recently, the Quakers and Abolitionists and groups that mightily struggled for civil rights. They've raised generations from the stench of their tombs. But today the church remains by and large acculturated to the violence of the world. We are embedded in it. We bestow our blessing on it. We coexist with it in contentment. The church finds ourselves in the tension of a paradox—we are at peace with war, injustice, and death.

We're akin to the professional mourners who come to Bethany. We go about fulfilling our religious obligations and keeping the big business of religion on the right track. On the other hand, we turn a blind eye toward the culture's proclivity to decimate the world's poor.

It stings to hear it. But we need to be honest about our failures. The demands of the Gospel are clear. It falls to us to fulfill the momentous commandments of Jesus.

But know this, as well, the church's crisis is not new. It dates back seventeen hundred years to the Constantinian arrangement when Rome assimilated Christianity into its empire. Christianity became imperial, coercive, dictatorial. And it soon found embarrassing the nonviolence outlined in the Sermon on the Mount. Nonviolence was discarded in favor of a theory of just war—a house of cards that rarely forestalls any wars. Before long, the church raised its own armies—Crusaders who eagerly waged war and killed others in the name of the nonviolent Jesus. Throughout Christendom, the centuries *Anno Domini* bulge with episodes of war, slavery, fleecing of the poor, and churchmen burning women at the stake. The church has outpaced the very Pharisees in cooperating with empire. In my estimation, our infidelity peaked with the institutional church's support of the Nazis. Most Lutherans and Catholics supported the regime. They did what they were told, acceded to the faithful going off to invade Poland, France, and Russia.

Above all, church leaders value order and control. And Hitler the sociopath guaranteed both so long as the church supported the Reich, permitted compromises to their theology, and remained silent as millions went to their deaths. The church's institutional survival rose in importance above the Gospel itself. And the church was overtaken by a bitter irony—the church, in essence, died. It became as deathly as the institutions around it.

Of course, thousands of heroic Christians did resist Nazism, such as Sophie Scholl, Franz Jägerstätter, and Alfred Delp. Theirs are the names—not the anonymous hierarchs who would survive at all costs—that we hold up as exemplars of a living Christianity in the twenty-first century.

The church has little changed today. The church today discounts Jesus' commandments by supporting war, dictatorships, oligarchies, and the military training of our young, and by ignoring the racism and sexism of its leaders. The Roman Catholic Church's recent sex-abuse scandal proves the case. Priests violate young people, and bishops and cardinals cover up to save face. Refusing to admit its own violence, the church ends up cooperating with the culture of death. And dies itself—indeed, one thinks, that part of it should die.

Along the same vein, during these years of aggression toward Iraq and Afghanistan, few priests or bishops have spoken out. Presumably out of fear that if they do, their parishioners would lodge complaints. For the sake of control and orderliness, the wars rage on and the priests and ministers keep silent. The Gospel does not exist in a vacuum. It comes to life precisely in such times as these.

Alas, the Gospel is declared all but dead when hundreds of priests serve in the military as chaplains of death. In such a position they unwittingly trace a cross over the dark ethic of war. Any hope of their teaching nonviolence, of their non-cooperating with war, lies quite off the map.

As a notorious example, the Jesuits assigned a priest to minister at Abu Graib prison, the torture center in Iraq staffed by U.S. soldiers. His role wasn't to expose torture or give solace to the tortured or stop the inhumanity for Christ's sake. His role was to offer Mass and consolation—to the torturers.

Catholic and other Christian campuses coast to coast offer the military free reign through such programs as the R.O.T.C. Seemingly, all our denominations have offered up their youth to the science of killing on behalf of the United States government.

The town of Los Alamos, New Mexico, birthplace of the bomb, is a case study in our cooperation with the culture of death. A modern-day Bethany, nearly all its inhabitants are given over to the power of death, pursuing their livelihood by designing the next generation of the nuclear bomb. Most are Christian, a good many Roman Catholic.

At the Catholic Church of the Immaculate Heart of Mary, right off Trinity Avenue and Oppenheimer Way, the priest blesses their work as God's will. He enjoys the backing of the archbishop of the diocese of Santa Fe. We've wrangled over this more than once, he and I.

The church, I say, has strayed from the Gospel. We need these weapons, he argues. I counter: it is our job to free the whole world over from the ways of death, to love our enemies. Nuclear weapons are our only security from rogue nations, he returns.

Being archbishop, he gets the last word. But the exchange is revealing. It goes to show that the Constantinian arrangement is alive and well. We are a contemporary version of professional mourners. We weep and pray while we fail to non-cooperate with our nation's stampeding toward death. God help us, we even regard one's participation as a religious vocation.

This obsession with order and control! Without realizing, the church has thrown its loyalty to the false gods of war. The God of life has receded from the church's mind. The God of resurrection has become largely irrelevant. We're no longer a church of peace, but of violence. No longer of new life, but of war.

But we are not bereft of hope. Into this predicament comes the nonviolent Jesus calling louder than ever: Take away the stone! Come forth, Lazarus! Unbind humanity and let it go free!

Listen for him. Take up the challenge to renounce cooperation with the cultures that rely on violence and death. Happily embrace Jesus' prerequisites of nonviolence. Create communities that uphold life. Worship the God of unconditional love and boundless peace.

Call one another out of the lucrative business of weapons designing and warmaking. The time for politesse is over. Frankly name our worst institutions as demonic and possessed. Point the way forward toward a new culture of life, nonviolence, justice, and love.

Church leaders, relinquish your tight grasp on absolute control. Trust the Holy Spirit to lead you to form new movements for disarmament and justice. You are the ones who should be leading us into true repentance for our complicity with violence and into the practice of Gospel nonviolence.

It is time for us to name the church as the peacemaking, life-giving community of followers of the nonviolent Jesus. To see the church as the place where life is celebrated, all are welcomed, everyone is reconciled, and Gospel nonviolence is taught. Dr. King defined the church as "the place you go from." If that's true, then the church should send us forth into the culture of violence on a mission to transform the planet into a new world of nonviolence.

The church has a glorious role: to take away the stone from the tomb, call out humanity from its tombs, and unbind everyone so that they might live in the freedom of life and peace. As the church fulfills this mission, it will rise and give Jesus cause once again to break into thanks.

Chapter 13

BEN SALMON, DOROTHY STANG, AND OSCAR ROMERO: THREE WHO FULFILLED JESUS' COMMANDMENTS

Read the lives of the saints, martyrs, prophets, and peace makers, and you'll encounter tales of faithful people who resisted death, called humanity from the tombs, and unbound those stuck in the culture of violence and war. History brims with shining examples. Here I present three—Ben Salmon, a World War I conscientious objector; Dorothy Stang, a nun gunned down for defending the Amazon region and its poor; and Oscar Romero, archbishop of San Salvador, heroic "voice for the voiceless."

Ben Salmon and His Army of Peace

Whenever my spirits sag over the apparently dim prospects for peace, I think of Ben Salmon, Catholic layman, husband, father, peacemaker, war resister, and World War I conscientious objector. His was a lonely, steadfast stretch of discipleship to the non-violent Jesus. I think of Ben and take heart once more.

Long before Mahatma Gandhi, Franz Jägerstätter, Dorothy Day, Dr. King, or Thomas Merton—before the Catholic Worker or Pax Christi or Vatican II or the U.S. Bishops' Pastoral Letter on Peace—this lone man stood and said that because of Jesus, he would not be a soldier. Right here in the United States. The story begins on April 6, 1917. It was the day President Wilson, the "peace president," declared war on Germany. The next day, Congress ratified the decision, bringing the United States into World War I. Two weeks later, Cardinal Gibbons of Baltimore, the de facto head of the U.S. Catholic Church, issued a letter to this effect: all Catholics were to support the war.

The letter was soon followed by the founding of the U.S. Bishops' National Catholic War Council, which set out to mobilize Catholics for, what it called, "war work." According to historians, the War Council led to the creation of the U.S. Catholic Conference of Bishops—a college of bishops not unlike the Judean leaders of Jesus' day. They too couldn't think past the logic of violence.

As war fever descended on nearly everyone, on June 5, 1917, twenty-eight-year-old Ben Salmon took up his pen.[*] He wrote the president, saying he would refuse to fight. "Regardless of nationality," he wrote,

All men are my brothers. God is "our father who art in heaven." The commandment "Thou shalt not kill" is unconditional and inexorable.... The lowly Nazarene taught us the doctrine of non-resistance, and so convinced was he of the soundness of that doctrine that he sealed his belief with death on the cross. When human law conflicts with Divine law, my duty is clear.

---

[*]For further information, see Torin Finney, *Unsung Hero of the Great War: The Life and Witness of Ben Salmon* (New York: Paulist Press, 1989); and "The Life and Witness of Ben Salmon," *The Catholic Peace Fellowship* 6, no. 1 (Spring 2007), available at *www.catholicpeacefellowship.org.*

Conscience, my infallible guide, impels me to tell you that prison, death, or both, are infinitely preferable to joining any branch of the Army.

A brave statement in those days. Congress, caught up in the fever, wasted little time getting a new law on the books. It outlawed activities "detrimental to the war effort"—public anti-war statements, anti-war literature, utterances that might encourage draft resistance—all these punishable by up to twenty years behind bars.

Under the law, the authorities arrested hundreds, harassed thousands. And when challenged, finally, the law was upheld by the Supreme Court.

Salmon had voted for Wilson. Like most, he had expected the president to lead the country to peace. And when the brilliant and upright candidate came to power and unleashed war, Salmon's disappointment burned deep. Wilson outdid even his hawkish predecessors in warmaking. (A pattern, need it be added, quite obvious today.)

Undeterred by the chill in the air, Ben rose to leadership in Denver's People's Council for Democracy and Peace, a national anti-war organization. In defiance of the law, he wrote letters, gave speeches, and distributed pamphlets. Soon he caught the attention of the *New York Times,* which hotly denounced him. He had become notorious.

Meantime the gears of war turned, going full tilt to unearth prospective recruits. On Christmas Day, Ben's army registration questionnaire arrived, which Ben returned, unfilled-out, accompanied by a letter explaining why. "Let those that believe in wholesale violation of the commandment, 'Thou Shalt not Kill' make a profession of faith by joining the army of war. I am in the army of peace, and in this army, I intend to live and die."

On January 15, 1918, Denver policemen arrived at his door. The papers hurled slander his way. The Knights of Columbus, the prominent Catholic lay association, in a fit of indignation, revoked his membership. In March he was tried and convicted. And then the sentence came down: nine months in the county jail.

Matters, already grim, spiraled downward quickly. While out on appeal, his draft notice arrived. Report for induction, it ordered, in three days. A second refusal, a second arrest. And this time he found himself in the clutches of the military authorities, who hustled him into solitary confinement at Fort Logan, Colorado.

At Fort Logan he was ordered to work. Again he refused. What to do about this, a troublemaker in their midst? Guards and other prisoners nearly lynched him that night. And so the authorities put him in chains and trundled him to Camp Funston in Kansas. There, they told him, he would face court martial for "desertion and propaganda." For desertion? "I've never actually been inducted," he said. No matter.

The preliminary hearing was held in Iowa, and an offer of leniency offered, a kind of quid pro quo. Again, no. He would make no deals with the military. He would rather face court martial—and defend himself. It was held on July 24, 1918, and in his own defense he argued three points. (1) He had been inducted illegally; (2) he was responsible for a dependent wife and mother; and (3) conscription violated the First and Fifth Amendments.

The court found him guilty; the verdict came down in minutes. The sentence . . . was death.

Second thoughts came to the court, and before long they commuted the sentence. He would spend twenty-five years at Fort Leavenworth, there be put to hard labor. More second thoughts came and lures and enticements. Be a legal clerk in an army office, they offered, and no more troubles. All charges dropped. His wife, having just given birth, urged him to accept, but the recalcitrant Ben again said no. Even non-combatant service, he said, entails cooperating with an institution "antithetical to Christianity." He would not cooperate with the culture of death.

They hauled him under guard to Leavenworth. He arrived on October 9, 1918, and a month later an armistice was declared. The war was over. But not for Ben; his imprisonment had just begun.

He was assigned to a unit comprised of hundreds of COs and there, with them, expected to work. He was quickly consigned to "The Hole"—solitary confinement—when he refused all orders. Five months he suffered in a dark, rat-infested cell. No toilet but a pail, bread and water his only food.

Matters grew worse yet, when in June 1919 the authorities transferred him to a military prison in Utah, where sadistic guards took a dim view of conscientious objectors. The guards inflicted beatings, withheld food, and kept them underdressed against the cold.

Still, he refused to buckle, and instead pushed things to their logical conclusion. A hunger strike. He wrote to the secretary of war: "Unless you [release me], you will cause my death from starvation, for I cannot honestly continue to support [the Greek war god] Mars as I have in the past. I now realize that even the tiny bit of assistance that I was rendering in the way of accepting your food was too much."

And he added: "Christ's doctrine to overcome evil with good" is the "most effective solution for individual and societal ills that has ever been formulated. It is a practical policy. . . . My life, my family, everything is now in the hands of God. His will be done."

Two weeks later, death loomed, and he asked to see a priest. The priest arrived, but refused to offer him Communion, hear his confession, or anoint him. Two other priests arrived some days later. And, after sizing things up, one of them agreed to the request for Communion. When word made its way back to the diocese, a fury descended. The priest was sent packing. Off to minor and punitive assignments in Oregon for pitying a traitor. Another instance of church colluding with the warmongering state.

Force-feeding followed—135 days of it—and then a one-way ticket to Washington, D.C., to St. Elizabeth's Hospital for the Insane.

While there he refused to languish; he kept busy—thinking, praying, and writing. From the ACLU archives we have the fruits of Ben's efforts, a two hundred-page, single-spaced essay on the fallacy of the just war. Much of it a refutation of the *Catholic Encyclopedia*'s article on war by "Father Macksey," a Jesuit from the Gregorian University in Rome. Point by point Ben refutes the lofty scholar.

"Either Christ is a liar or war is never necessary, and very properly assuming that Christ told the truth, it follows that the State is without [in the words of Father Macksey] 'judicial authority to determine when war is necessary,' because it is never necessary."

Much of Salmon's thinking depended on the Apostle Paul. "Overcome evil with good," admonished Paul (Rom. 12:21).

We do not attempt to overcome lying with lies; we overcome it with truth. We do not try to overcome curses with curses, but we overcome with silence or with words of friendship. Sickness is not overcome with sickness; it is overcome with health. . . . Anger is overcome with meekness, pride by humility. And the successful way to overcome the evil of war is by the good of peace, a steadfast refusal to render evil for evil.

A sad matter when faithfulness, nonviolence, and sanity are regarded, as they were in Jesus' own day, as insanity.

Eventually, in the cultural mind there passed a softening of unbending feelings. The newly formed ACLU had ignored his many pleas for help, but gradually it changed its tune. The *New York Times*, previously Ben's sharp detractor, wrote about his plight and hunger strike. The well-respected Monsignor John Ryan of Catholic University got wind of the news and personally lobbied the secretary of war.

The War Department, in a feeble way, finally relented: it would release thirty-three conscientious objectors. Ben would be among them. Thanksgiving 1920 he was released and, from the army he never joined, dishonorably discharged. The news made front pages across the nation.

Persona non grata thereafter, he struggled to find good work. And when the Depression set in, he and his family landed in deep poverty. His health never recovered—the forced feedings had taken their toll—and in 1932 he caught pneumonia and died.

The life and times of Ben Salmon, all but unheard of in our day and age.

The Sign of Peace, a newsletter of the Catholic Peace Fellowship, a group that promotes conscientious objection, concludes that Ben Salmon wasn't just a faithful Catholic, but a "confessor of the faith." I would go farther. I regard him as a saint for the ages. He took on the nation; he took on Christendom. He took them on in reverence toward the Christ of peace. He shows us what allegiance to the nonviolent Jesus looks like.

Little has changed since Ben's life and death struggle. Among the military, a third is Catholic. Vastly more theologians than not, like Father Macksey, support a moral justification of war, even nuclear deterrence. I get the feeling the bishops would like to start a new National Catholic War Council; they certainly haven't formed a "Peace Council." And today, as in Ben's own day, an eloquent president elected on promises of peace, has taken warmaking to new heights. The times, Ben's and ours, run parallel. And that being the case, one of the brightest beacons we have is Ben.

Dorothy Stang, Martyr for the Poor and the Earth

On February 12, 2005, Sr. Dorothy Stang walked along a dirt road deep in the heart of Brazil's Amazon on her way to meet a handful of poor farmers bearing up under harassment from illegal loggers and ranchers. She trudged along, until two hired assassins blocked her way. In response to their challenge, she produced maps and documents proving that the government had designated the land as a reserve for the landless poor. "Do you have a weapon?" they asked. Yes, she answered, showing them the Bible she carried for decades. She opened it and began to read aloud: "Blessed are the poor in spirit. Blessed are those who hunger and thirst for justice. Blessed are the peacemakers. . . . " Then, she said, "God bless you, my sons."

The two shot her six times and fled. Her body lay on the dirt road all day, nearby witnesses later said, because they were afraid they would be shot if they moved it. As it rained, her blood mixed with the dirt.

The news pierced me to the core. I felt the same stab of pain and glory as when I heard the news on December 3, 1980, that four U.S. churchwomen—Ita Ford, Maura Clarke, Dorothy Kazel, and Jean Donovan—were missing in El Salvador. Their raped and murdered bodies were discovered the following day.

I suspected early on that Sr. Dorothy had attained great moral heights. Anyone who leaves homeland, spends four decades serving the poorest of the poor in the Amazon, and defends the rain forest—long before anyone ever thought of an environmental movement—must possess enormous commitment, faith, and vision.

She was born in Dayton in 1931, one of nine in a lively and devout Catholic family. At seventeen, she entered the Sisters of Notre Dame de Namur, and in 1953 she was sent to serve the poor, teach children, and assist at Most Holy Trinity parish in the desert of Sunnyslope, Arizona. After many good years, she volunteered to join a mission to Brazil, and in 1966 off she went—later to become a citizen there. In the years before she was killed, she was hailed for her work. She learned the languages and set up remote parishes. She walked the forest and met with the poorest farmers. She set up dozens of base communities and taught them the Gospel. She launched twenty-three schools and created a structure for the poor to reclaim their land. A tidy sum of work. She helped spawn the base community movement, liberation theology, and the environmental movement.

Feisty and energetic and loving, one of the great saints. Surely she'll be canonized one day. She remained faithful to the poor, to the beleaguered Amazon, and so to the Gospel and the God of life and liberation. Beautiful stories are now being passed on. How she fed the hungry, built community, lived in destitution. How she confronted illegal loggers and corrupt ranchers, the class that stole the poor's land, kept them in misery, and bought off the police, the military, and the government.

Death threats had rained down on Dorothy for years, along with insults and hate mail. Ranchers took aim at the community center for women that she had founded and riddled it with bullets. On one occasion the police arrested her for passing out "subversive" material. It was the United Nations Universal

Declaration of Human Rights. Another time, she escaped by a hair's-breadth an attempt on her life.

Yet she carried on and included the ranchers in her prayers for peace. Her defense of the poor was fearless. She did her homework, studied the laws, and barged repeatedly into government offices to lodge heated complaints. The poor, she said, were promised land, but here they are being driven off, loggers and ranchers behind it all, and the government turning a blind eye. Turning a blind eye, as well, toward the destruction of the forest. She stood fearless even as she witnessed over the years the marriage of powers, commercial interests, and the military. Together they threatened and terrorized and forced many of her programs to collapse. But she remained positive and hopeful, always smiling.

"That I've been able to live with, love, be loved by, and work with the Brazilian people, to help them find confidence in themselves, to profoundly sense God's presence in their lives and then be a creative influence in society from which a more human society can be born, I thank all of you," she wrote her family and friends on her sixtieth birthday in 1991. "It's a chain reaction. We can give positive input-energy into life—but we need to be charged also. In the midst of all this violence there are many small communities that have learned the secret of life: sharing, solidarity, confidence, equality, pardon, working together. God is present—generator and sustainer of all life. Thus life is productive and transforming in the midst of all this."

Over the years, Dorothy wore a favorite T-shirt, which read: "The death of the forest is the end of our lives." She knew firsthand what the destruction of the Amazon meant, not only for Brazil but for the planet. In 1991, she took a sabbatical program in Oakland, California, to study creation spirituality with Matthew Fox. Afterward, she attended the historic 1992 first Earth

Summit in Rio de Janeiro. A few weeks later, she wrote her family, "Tell all that we must make great efforts to save our planet. Mother Earth is not able to provide anymore. Her water and air are poisoned and her soil is dying of exaggerated use of chemicals, all in the name of profit. Pray for all of us and for a world where all can live—plants, animals, and humans—in peace and harmony."

In 2002, the death threats intensified. The mayor of the nearby town said, "We have to get rid of that woman if we are going to have peace." A list circulated of people with "bounties" on their heads. Atop the list was her name—Stang: $20,000.

But she was undeterred. "I know that they want to kill me," she said, "but I will not go away. My place is here alongside these people who are constantly humiliated by the powerful."

Visiting her family and community in Ohio a few months before she was killed, she told one sister, "I just want to sink myself into God." Her absence gave the authorities space to work a different tack. On her return she was met with a trumped-up charge, organizing armed rebellion. This should put her in her place, water down her gumption. And off to trial she went. It was in the middle of it that she was killed. "I look at Jesus carrying the cross," she said a few days before her death when asked by a novice about her prayer, "and I ask for the strength to carry the suffering of the people." A day before her death, she said: "If something is going to happen, I hope it happens to me, because the others have families to care for."

At her funeral two thousand people marched. Hundreds of reporters descended from around the world. "Today, we are not going to bury Dorothy. We are going to plant her," her community said. "Dorothy vive!" the crowd returned.

Brazil's president announced days later the creation of two new national parks in the rain forest. He declared the expansion of another and placed eight and a half million acres more under environmental protection. And he suspended logging in the most hotly contested areas.

Throughout her life and in her martyrdom, Dorothy unbound the poor and set them free. Her defense of the earth and its poor was a true work of liberation. Like Jesus, she was killed for her work. But like Jesus, she is rising in her people and in the land. In us, too, if we join her campaign.

Archbishop Oscar Romero, Voice for the Voiceless

"I have often been threatened with death," Archbishop Oscar Romero told a Guatemalan reporter two weeks before his assassination on March 24, 1980. "If they kill me, I shall arise in the Salvadoran people. If the threats come to be fulfilled, from this moment I offer my blood to God for the redemption and resurrection of El Salvador. Let my blood be a seed of freedom and the sign that hope will soon be reality."

Oscar Romero gave his life in the hope that peace and justice would one day become a reality in El Salvador. He called the people forth and urged them to turn their backs on a culture that condoned death squads. He now lives on in all those who carry on the nonviolent struggle for justice and peace.

Romero spent his years up until 1977 as a quiet, pious, conservative cleric. Indeed, while bishop he sided with the greedy landlords, important powerbrokers, and violent death squads. When he became archbishop, the radical Jesuits at the university in San Salvador were crushed. They immediately wrote him off—all but one, Rutilio Grande, who reached out to Romero in the weeks after his installation and urged him to learn from the poor and speak on their behalf.

Grande himself was a giant for social justice. He organized the rural poor in Aguilares and paid for it with his life on March 12,

1977. Standing over Grande's dead body that night, Romero was transformed into one of the world's great champions for the poor and oppressed. From then on, he denounced every act of violence, injustice, and war. He became a fiery prophet of justice and peace, "the voice of the voiceless." In Jon Sobrino's words, "a new Jeremiah." For me, Romero was a sign of God's active presence in the world, a living symbol of the struggle for justice and what the church could be.

The day after Grande's death, Romero preached a sermon that stunned El Salvador. With the force of Martin Luther King Jr., Romero defended Grande, demanded social and economic justice for the poor, and called everyone to take up Grande's prophetic work. To protest the government's participation in the murders, Romero closed the parish school for three days and cancelled all Masses in the country the following week, except for one special Mass in the cathedral.

That act alone would have put Romero in the annals of history. Imagine if every Mass in the United States but one had been canceled in protest after the death of Dr. King! Over one hundred thousand people attended the cathedral Mass that Sunday and heard Romero's bold call for justice, disarmament, and peace. Grande's life and death bore good fruit in the heart and soul of Romero. Suddenly the nation had a towering figure in its midst.

Within months, priests, catechists, and church workers were targeted and assassinated, so Romero spoke out even more forcefully. He even criticized the president, which no Salvadoran bishop had ever done before, and few in the hemisphere ever did. As El Salvador's U.S.-backed death squads attacked villages and churches and massacred campesinos, Romero's truth-telling became a veritable subversive campaign of nonviolent civil disobedience.

Soon Romero was greeted with applause everywhere he went. Thousands wrote to him regularly, telling their stories, thanking him for his prophetic voice and sharing their new-found courage. His Sunday homilies were broadcast nationwide on live radio. The country came to a standstill every time he spoke. Everyone listened, even the death squads. He said, in effect: "Lazarus, come forth!"

As Romero's stature grew and his leadership for justice and peace deepened, his simple faith and devotion gave him the foundation from which he could take on the forces of death. To protest the government's silence in the face of recent massacres, he refused to attend the inauguration of the new Salvadoran president. The church, he announced, is "not to be measured by the government's support but rather by its own authenticity, its evangelical spirit of prayer, trust, sincerity, and justice, its oppo-sition to abuses." While he embodied the prophetic role of the church, he also modeled that spirit of prayer, trust, and sincerity in his everyday life.

As the arrests, torture, disappearances, and murders con-tinued, Romero made two unprecedented decisions. First, on Easter Monday 1978, he opened the seminary in downtown San Salvador to welcome any and all displaced victims of violence. Hundreds of homeless, hungry, and brutalized people moved into the seminary, transforming the quiet religious retreat into a crowded, noisy shelter, makeshift hospital, and playground. (I worked there for a few days in 1985 and tried to imagine a simi-lar gesture in the United States. Never in the United States have church leaders made such an offer.)

Next, he halted construction on San Salvador's new cathe-dral. When the war is over, the hungry are fed, and the children are educated, then we can resume building our cathedral, he said. Both were historic initiatives, and they stunned the other bishops, cast judgment on the Salvadoran government, and lifted the people's spirits.

Meanwhile, Romero's preaching reached biblical heights. "Like a voice crying in the desert," he said, "we must continually say *no* to violence and *yes* to peace." His August 1978 pastoral letter outlined the evils of "institutional violence" and repression and advocated "the power of nonviolence that today has conspicuous students and followers.... The counsel of the Gospel to turn the other cheek to an unjust aggressor, far from being passive or cowardly," he wrote, "shows great moral force that leaves the aggressor morally overcome and humiliated. The Christian always prefers peace to war."

Romero lived in a sparse, three-room hermitage on the grounds of a hospital run by a community of nuns. During his busy days, he traveled the country, met with hundreds of poor Salvadorans, presided at Mass, and met with local community leaders. He assisted everyone he could. Later, he said that one of his primary duties as archbishop had become not just challenging the U.S.-backed government and its death squads, but claiming the dead bodies of their victims, including priests, nuns, and catechists.

On one of my visits, a Salvadoran told me how Romero would drive out to city garbage dumps to look among the trash for the discarded, tortured victims of the death squads on behalf of grieving relatives. "These days I walk the roads gathering up dead friends, listening to widows and orphans, and trying to spread hope," he said.

In particular, Romero took time to speak with the dozens of people threatened every day by government death squads. People lined up at his office to ask for help and protection, to complain about harassment and death threats, and to find some support and guidance in their time of grief and struggle.

Romero received and listened to everyone. His compassionate ear fueled his prophetic voice.

By late 1979 and early 1980, his Sunday sermons issued his strongest calls yet for conversion to justice and an end to the massacres. "To those who bear in their hands or in their conscience the burden of bloodshed, of outrages, of the victimized, innocent or guilty, but still victimized in their human dignity, I say: Be converted. You cannot find God on the path of torture. God is found on the way of justice, conversion, and truth."

When President Jimmy Carter announced in February 1980 that he was going to increase U.S. military aid to El Salvador by millions of dollars a day, Romero was shocked. He wrote a long public letter to Carter, asking the United States to cancel all military aid. Carter ignored Romero's plea and sent the aid. Between 1980 and 1992, the United States spent $6 billion. In the same span more than seventy-five thousand people were killed.

In the weeks afterwards, the killings increased. So did the death threats against Romero. He made a private retreat, prepared for his death, discovered an even deeper peace, and mounted the pulpit. During his March 23, 1980, Sunday sermon, Romero let loose and issued one of the greatest appeals for peace and disarmament in church history:

I would like to make an appeal in a special way to the men of the army, to the police, to those in the barracks. Brothers, you are part of our own people. You kill your own campesino brothers and sisters. And before an order to kill that a man may give, the law of God must prevail that says: Thou shalt not kill! No soldier is obliged to obey an order against the law of God. No one has to fulfill an immoral law. It is time to recover your consciences and to obey your consciences rather than the orders of sin. The church, defender of the rights of God, of the law of God, of human dignity, the dignity of the person, cannot remain silent before such abomination. We want the government to take seriously that reforms are worth nothing when they come about stained with so much blood. In the name of God, and in the name of this suffering people whose laments rise to heaven each day more tumultuously, I beg you, I ask you, I order you in the name of God: Stop the repression!

The next day, March 24, 1980, Romero presided over a small evening Mass in the chapel of the hospital compound where he lived, in honor of a beloved woman who had died a year before. He read from John's Gospel: "Unless the grain of wheat falls to the earth and dies, it remains only a grain. But if it dies, it bears much fruit" (12:23–26). Then he preached about the need to give our lives for others as Christ did. Just as he concluded, he was shot in the heart by a man standing in the back of the church. He fell behind the altar and collapsed at the foot of a huge crucifix depicting a bloody and bruised Christ. His blood drenched his vestments and pooled on the floor. He gasped for breath and died in minutes.

Romero's funeral became the largest demonstration in Salvadoran history, some say in the history of Latin America. The government was so afraid of the grieving people that they threw bombs into the crowd and opened fire, killing some thirty and injuring hundreds more. The Mass of Resurrection was never completed and Romero was hastily buried.

One recent biography of Pope John Paul II reveals that he had decided to remove Romero as archbishop of San Salvador. In fact, he signed the removal order on the morning of March 24. In some ways, I'm grateful that Romero never lived to hear of that dreadful news. His martyrdom continues to transform the church and the world.

Today we remember Oscar Romero as a saint and a martyr, as a champion of the poor and prophet of justice. He calls us to live in solidarity with the poor and oppressed, to think with them, feel with them, walk with them, listen to them, serve them, stand with them, become one with them, and even die with them. Put shortly, Romero's voice still summons us to fulfill Jesus' last commandment, "Unbind them and set them free."

Archbishop Oscar Romero gives us one of the best examples in history of fulfilling the commandments of Jesus. As we join his life-giving work, Romero rises in us, as does Christ, and we too enter the fullness of life.

Chapter 14

THE PLOT TO KILL
THE NONVIOLENT JESUS

Jesus raises his friend from the tomb, and the old disheartening adage falls like a hammer: no good deed goes unpunished.

"From that day on, they planned to put him to death."

Some who had gathered in Bethany begin to believe. "But some went to the Pharisees and told them what Jesus had done." Alarmed, the Pharisees and chief priests convene the Sanhedrin, the ruling council. John is referring to the religious leaders. On a visceral level they know their authority and privilege are at stake. Their coercive powers too. Who will bow and cower before them if someone goes around liberating the people from the fear of death? It can't be permitted. Jesus will put them out of business.

And so they gather in their august hall. "What are we going to do? This man is performing many signs. If we leave him alone, all will believe in him, and the Romans will come and take away both our land and our nation."

Here John offers us a slice of wit and irony. Rome did precisely what the rulers feared. The Romans overran Jerusalem in 70 C.E. Not because of destiny, not because the will of a capricious God. But, insinuates John, it was because the rulers had refused Jesus' gift of life and nonviolence. Put briefly: Sell yourself to the patronage of empire and it will eventually rise up against you. Or according to the familiar proverb Jesus coined: "Live by the sword, die by the sword." The rulers deliberate around the table, and their dialog rings true to life. It was Caiaphas, the high priest, who argued against Jesus, hewing the classic line of the "scapegoat principle."

"You do not understand that it is better for you that one man should die for the people, so that the whole nation may not perish."

The scapegoat principle: it lies at the bottom of all violence. It is nearly instinctual among us and has driven every culture down through the ages. Throughout history, empires have relied on it to try to crush liberation movements. All that is needed is to stir the crowd's frenzy against the stranger, the noncomformist—in this instance, the charismatic leader of the dispossessed.

The rulers figure his subversive campaign will suffer a great setback and in the bargain the people will unite around his demise. Mobbing the scapegoat always creates a moment of counterfeit oneness. (Mark's Gospel makes the same point through caricature. The mocking of Jesus on the cross is unanimous—including even the two crucified with him. Killing the scapegoat provides a catharsis and creates a moment of accord.)

Caiaphas's logic has been seized by authorities in our own century. Mahatma Gandhi, Martin Luther King, Steve Biko, and many others have died by the subterfuge, behind the scenes, of shadowy figures in power. Their argument: "It is better for one person to die." Always, they say, to preserve nation and land.

But violence ultimately fails. Relying on violence only spawns a new wave of it. In Jesus' time the next wave arose with the Zealots (guerrillas against the occupation) and the so-called

Sicarii (assassins of Jews who collaborated with Rome). Rome retaliated in turn, destroying both nation and land.

Jesus chose a nobler way. Cultures of death will eventually succumb to creative nonviolence. Break the cycle of violence, he taught his followers. Give your lives if need be to pioneer this new way of life. He summed it up like this: "Offer no violent resistance to one who does evil" (Matt. 5:37). Should this catch on, should its simplicity and brilliance capture enough minds, rebels will cease killing, religious authorities will cease killing, oppressors will cease killing. And empires will put away imperial claims. Jesus sows seeds of nonviolent transformation and lasting peace. A kind of heaven on earth.

But the authorities are blind; they act predictably and clumsily. Ironically, by striking down the One who embodied resurrection and life, they unleash the Spirit of nonviolence that beckons people to this day. For Jesus didn't only die, he was raised in vindication. The first Easter ushered in the ultimate nonviolent revolution, a spiritual eruption that, if harnessed, can bring down every empire, transform every nation, and spread justice wide.

John the evangelist understands. He knows the dynamic of nonviolence. And he can perceive in advance the inevitable outcome. Through Jesus' nonviolent love, his death and resurrection, he will save the nation—and from there all nations—"and gather into one the dispersed children of God." This ingathering goes on to this day. It is God's yearning to disarm us, raise us, and set us to work gathering the human race into one family of peace. The vision burns in the evangelist's mind.

Meantime the rulers planned how they might put Jesus to death. No longer now could Jesus go about in public. So he and his disciples laid low in the village of Ephraim. As for the crowds in Jerusalem, they buzzed with gossip. Would he attend the approaching Passover or not? Voyeurs and rumormongers, they thrilled at the idea of the big showdown. Indeed, the authorities had issued a decree. "If anyone knew where he was, he should inform them. . . . "

Jesus now is chief among wanted men. One presumes bounty hunters are keeping out a weather eye. Here is the rulers' big chance to put an end to him and his movement that dares undermine their violent ways. They want no gift of life to challenge their power. They can brook no spreading of belief among people yearning for freedom. They can tolerate no change; they dismiss Jesus' ideas as fantasy and mischief.

As for the people, many prefer their subjection to the authorities, knowing it's a life unworthy of humans, fully expecting to die one day in misery. They are addicted to despair. They turn away from Jesus' offer of *agape*, selfless love and boundless compassion.

"There is no greater love than to lay down one's life for one's friends," he says the night before they finally kill him. His compassionate love, so to say, is the protagonist of the story. It drives his offer of new life to the beleaguered world. It extends to everyone, not only to Lazarus but to those who had taken up stones against him and the religious authorities and imperial soldiers who eventually do away with him. Jesus yearns to free everyone.

This love running through the story should challenge our own narrow practice of love. When Jesus raises Lazarus at the risk of his own life, he inspires us to widen our own hearts, to reach out with the same selfless love, to take bold action to liberate each other into the new life of peace. As we expand our compassion and widen our embrace to help everyone—including our enemies—our faith, hope, and love will deepen and we will find new strength to bear any cost for our loving action.

But Jesus offers this love for another reason, as well: to honor God who champions life. Jesus calls our attention back to the Creator, who we begin to understand, is neither parochial nor vengeful. God's compassion is boundless. Our minds have been violated; our impressions of God have been wrong. They have been swayed by the culture of death, which invokes a god of anger. They lay claim to violence by conjuring a violent god. Benefitting from injustice they falsely teach that God is unjust. Or more to the point, that the injustice imputed to God is just. The rulers have created the divinity in their own image.

They decree that God sustains the system in which the few have immense power while most suffer in subjection, in which a minority are chosen for great wealth and the rest for distended bellies. In which a few are foreordained for luxury and the rest for early graves. Theirs is a god who oppresses the poor and turns away from the broken—and who doesn't shy away from crushing noble resisters. Priests and lawyers in service to power disfigured the image of God.

But of course our Gospel writer turns this evil characterization on its head. The God of Jesus is compassionate and life-giving. When Jesus raises Lazarus for the glory of God, he points humanity back to the true nature of God. God is a deity we can trust and enjoy. Our hearts can rejoice to know of God's commitment to everyone's good. A joy that will last forever.

Still, our peculiarity remains: we resist the gift. To this day humanity feels safer clinging to the deathliness of violent cultures. Our imaginations falter as to how trapped we are. And when we encounter anyone unbound and free, our scapegoating impulse begins to rise.

A dark irony. Anyone who points the way out of violence suffers the culture's wrath and sanctions. It's the only response a deathly culture knows: kill all who jeopardize its claim to kill. The empire and its acolytes regard their killing as the final word. The life that God offers they scoff at. And in their arrogance, they clothe themselves in godly trappings and frills.

What they fail to realize is that neither God's gift nor God's servants can be destroyed. Christ rises and the Christ within his followers rises, too. The nonviolent cannot be eternally crushed; they live on forever in the new life of resurrection. Their survival is guaranteed; they never die. The ultimate word from God is *life* and all its cognates.

Let us, then, study the saints, engage in the holy work of liberating humanity and, in good Ignatian style, ponder the story.

- Which character do we most resemble?

- Does some part of us respond with scorn toward those who demonstrate a resurrected life?

- Have we ever resonated with a group impulse to scapegoat?

- Is there a part of us drawn toward nonviolence?

- What risk are we willing to take to lead others, including our own religious authorities, into resurrection life?

- Where is *agape* leading us?

Such questions would be impossible without knowing that with Jesus, death does not get the last word; resurrection can be lived today. Jesus has gone before us; we know now where we are headed. With confidence, then, we can liberate our imaginations and entertain the penetrating questions. They are worth pondering.

Chapter 15

WASHING
EACH OTHER'S FEET

Jesus' days are numbered, the machinations are underway. But Jesus' exuberant living goes on. In his honor a party is given, a gathering in Bethany at Lazarus's house, where Lazarus "reclines at table with Jesus." Lazarus is co-honoree. The bright festivities later fall under something of a shadow—this when Mary takes "a liter of costly perfumed oil made of pure nard and [anoints] the feet of Jesus and [dries] them with her hair."

What does her gesture mean? It means more than mere welcome, more than sweet piety. By her gesture she prepares Jesus, who has just raised her brother, for his own impending death. A somber gesture in which she frankly acknowledges: his risking the cross is the only way. She's the first to understand. And Jesus gratefully receives her gesture, regarding it as a sacrament of support and affirmation.

Judas, on the other hand, regards it as something else: a waste. Under the pretext of giving alms to the poor, he would rather have seen the fat sum deposited in the community till, of which he was guardian—and, embezzler that he was, from which he stole. But Mary's extravagant gesture rings with authenticity and truth and Jesus defends her. "Leave her alone. Let her keep this for the day of my burial."

A day that is getting nearer. For word is out that Jesus is in Bethany, and the town fills with seekers and the curious. And seething, the authorities, trying to reestablish their prerogative, widen the dragnet. They drafted a death warrant on Lazarus of Bethany, as well.

Bethany. It's worth noting that the Gospel of Luke ends in Bethany (24:50–53). There the risen Jesus raises his hands and blesses his friends and disciples and ascends into heaven. They turn their gaze heavenward and "did him homage and returned to Jerusalem with great joy, and they were continually in the temple praising God." Bethany—place of death and resurrection, anointing and ascension, despair and hope, violence and nonviolence. It is the epicenter of contending forces, the place where God wrangles with death and prevails in glory.

The glory of Passover is drawing near: the festive remembrance of God's liberation. And Jesus enters the city to cries of "Hosanna! Blessed is he who comes in the name of the Lord!" The people wave palm branches like flags and toss them before the "king" bestriding a mule. One thinks the Gospel writer himself lost sight of the mockery implied in the scene. It is almost certain that during that same Passover, from another gate, accompanied by fanfare and acclamation, Herod Antipas and his arrayed entourage arrived, all on noble steeds bred for battle. And here is Jesus, he and the raggedy crowd engaging in spontaneous street theater mocking the trappings of power and the culture of death.

John downplays the mockery and rather crafts the scene as a fulfillment of the prophet Zechariah's heralding a non violent age.

Rejoice heartily, O daughter Zion. Shout for joy, O daughter Jerusalem! See, your king shall come to you, a just savior is he. Meek and riding on an ass, on a colt, the foal of an ass. He shall banish

the chariot from Ephraim, and the horse from Jerusalem. The
warrior's bow shall be banished, and he shall proclaim peace to
the nations. His dominion shall be from sea to sea, and from the
river to the ends of the earth. (Zech. 9:9–10)

Here comes the nonviolent Jesus! The crowds are shouting
"Hosanna," the Pharisees are throwing up their hands—"Look,
the whole world has gone after him"—and, as if to demonstrate
the point, heathen Greeks enter the scene. Might we, they ask,
have an audience with Jesus? It's an inquiry that serves as a sign.
Jesus realizes his hour has come. The day is near that he must
depart the world.

Time to prepare his cadre for what's to come and why.
"Unless a grain of wheat falls to the ground and dies, it remains
just a grain of wheat; but if it dies, it produces much fruit." He
is teaching them the mystery embedded in reality—heaven on
earth blossoms out of self-giving, life-giving love. Moreover:
"Whoever loves his life loses it, and whoever hates his life in
this world, will preserve it for eternal life." And then he issues
something in the nature of a summons: "Whoever serves me
must follow me, and where I am, there also will my servant be."

Here is nonviolent discipleship concisely expressed. Peace
isn't served by our hanging back. It's brought by giving our lives
in love with Jesus, in Jesus, through Jesus, and for Jesus.

Then he confesses a troubled soul, out of which he prays:
"Father, glorify your name." A peal of thunder returns from the
sky, the stentorian voice of the Almighty: "I have glorified it and
will glorify it again."

This is John's rendition of the Transfiguration. But here John
insinuates something besides. Throughout history, humanity
has corrupted God's justice and sullied the divine name. Now,
through Jesus, God's good name will be restored. Namely, when-

ever there is fullness of life and the terror of death banished, God's name is wreathed in glory.

And God passes the glory on. Jesus, light of the world, is glorified by God because of his being prepared to complete his mission, though it courts the Roman cross. And even there, on a cross, will Jesus be glorified. His suffering love carries the power to disarm everyone, because it is God's way to transform humanity. "When I am lifted up from the earth, I will draw everyone to myself." Jesus proceeds in the confidence that his way will win out. Everyone—*everyone*—will be taken into the new life of resurrection. Jesus' nonviolence will win over everyone who ever lived. Jesus is no hapless victim. He knows what he's doing and that with the God of peace all things are possible.

God assures him of eternal life. And us, too.

The Washing of the Feet

This theme of eternal life is carried over to the last supper and John's lengthy "last supper discourse," where Jesus offers his final reflections. But unlike in the Synoptics, which stress the bread and the wine, John's account features foot-washing (13:1–21). It's an episode so central to Holy Thursday liturgies that for centuries it has been wildly misunderstood. The episode is *not* meant to inspire us to service. It is *not* meant to urge us toward self-humiliation. Rather it is a ritual of preparing our feet to walk Jesus' road of nonviolence.

Think of it as a rite of passage of sorts, a summons to the holy lineage of *agape*, perhaps martyrdom and, beyond, resurrection. To enter upon such a life, ritual is in order. Ritual is how we prepare one another; it's how we spread mutual support. Disciples prepare one another's feet to tread the Way.

Mary of Bethany did the same for Jesus—not only symbolically to prepare him for burial, but to fortify him for his walk toward Jerusalem, where almost certainly he would face the cross. Apparently, just as Mary prepared Jesus, he decided to prepare his disciples. He learned from her, so he instructs them. Whoever follows him must be anointed for the difficult journey. There are bound to be consequences to resisting the injustices of empire. They wash one another's feet, they prepare themselves. They've chosen a road that could lead to martyrdom.

This is a political reading that is strange to our ears. All our lives an opposite reading has been hammered into our heads. Says Wes Howard-Brook in *Becoming Children of God* (Orbis, 1994):

> *How many Holy Thursday services and homilies have put priest and bowl before the congregation as an "example" of "lowering oneself like Jesus" to do the dirty work of washing feet. How easy it is for relatively safe and secure middle-class Christians to deny the call to death in favor of charity work!*

> *The prevailing interpretation is a function of both the chasm between the position of the interpreter and that of the Johannine community as well as the folly of taking passages out of context. If readers are comfortable, it is enough of a challenge to call them to serve the poor (or even "one another") by humble actions.*

> *But if readers are like the Johannine community—as people in El Salvador, Malawi, and other places are where proclaiming God's truth is to risk one's life— "humble service" is a commonplace that requires no exhortation at all. It is the call to help one another face death that is both the challenge and comfort of the Gospel.* (299–300)

Between the lines, says Howard-Brook, is "the risen Jesus, who lays down his life for his own, girding himself to prepare his disciples to see their own deaths that are approaching!"

The clues, Howard-Brook notes, lie in the verbs. "He *rose* from the supper and *laid down* his outer garments and *girded* himself. . . ." (13:14). A fine and subtle writer, this John the Evangelist. His paschal allusions conceal themselves among his verbs.

Understood correctly, foot-washing we're in dire need of. Practicing Gospel nonviolence, steadfastly resisting war and injustice, accepting the consequences including inevitable rejection, perhaps harassment, arrest, jailing, or dying—these require that we prepare one another. This fresh reading, I trust, will be a comfort. It should fortify us in our public work for justice and peace. We are not lost; neither are we bereft. Jesus has prepared us for the road to peace. "I have set the example," he said, "and you should do for each other exactly what I've done for you."

Jesus' final teachings, plus his hopes and dreams, are set down in the following several chapters. He calls his followers to keep his word, practice *agape* toward one another, and welcome the gift of peace. What we need for the journey he promises to give us. All we need to do is ask. And he concludes: be one. Exhibit to the world the unity of the human family, and one day, he assures us, our joy will be complete.

Beautiful and compelling, but to the very last, his disciples fail to comprehend. We see it that very night, when Judas guides Roman soldiers and Temple guards to the garden. When they seize Jesus, Simon Peter's instinct is to unsheathe his sword and lop off an ear of the high priest's slave. The episode rarely shocks us anymore—but it was meant to. Is the nonviolent Jesus to be defended through the violence of the sword? Obtuse Peter has absorbed very little. And Jesus must rebuke him: "Put your sword back in its scabbard!" Other versions read: "Stop! No more of this!"

It dawns on them now. Jesus will not allow himself to be defended through violence. They understand for the first time. Before their eyes he renounces violence, not only rhetorically, but when surrounded, when the circle closes. His kingdom rejects violence in practice. His disciples' reliance on it is forbidden.

Finally, they understand and . . . run away.

As for Simon Peter, nonviolence on actual display goes beyond his faculties: he denies knowing Jesus three times that night.

It is on this tragic night that the trial commences, a staged spectacle more than a trial. The fate of the accused is already sealed. "What accusation do you bring . . . ?" Pilate asks. The high priest's reasoning is circular. "If this man weren't a criminal we wouldn't have handed him over to you."

Our author the evangelist knows the outcome, but deft composer that he is, he frames the story so that the world doesn't judge Jesus so much as, through his trials, Jesus judges the world. "My kingdom," he testifies, "is not from this world. If my kingdom were from this world, my followers would fight . . . But my kingdom is not of this world" (18:36). Jesus draws a glaring distinction between his nonviolent kingdom and kingdoms of the powerful. Pilate sends him to his death ultimately, but Jesus' condemnation two millennia later still hangs in the air.

The torture is carried out and then the crucifixion. And just when one would expect him to knuckle under, his nonviolence shows itself as perfected. He neither recants nor retaliates. He utters, "It is finished." Jesus unites his suffering to the sufferings of humankind. Here is the divine showing us how to be human.

One can't help but wonder how, how die on the empire's cross without malice on the tongue? He can do it because he surrenders himself to God's loving hands. That, after all, is the key to practicing nonviolence, knowing God as the author of life and peace. Keep the focus on the God of love and all will be well, no matter what the violent culture does to us.

I offer a final observation. Uniquely and deliberately, John juxtaposes the last supper discourse with the passion story in which Jesus rejects violence. John draws us into the narrative and there forces us into a decision. For a thousand years the church has all but ignored the gravity of John's narrative strategy. And the consequence is predictable. We worship in churches that bless war, coddle the rich, and go on record as countenancing nuclear arms.

But John's nonviolent Jesus calls us nevertheless. He calls us out of our addiction to violence. He calls us into the freedom of resurrection, into the new life of peace and nonviolence.

Today.

Chapter 16

THE RESURRECTION OF THE NONVIOLENT JESUS

On the first morning of the week, Mary Magdalene arrives at the tomb to anoint Jesus' body—only to find an empty tomb. The story of Lazarus has come full circle. The One who called humanity from its tomb and died a subversive's death—he himself rose to new life. Once again an empty tomb.

She's puzzled—what foul play is this?—and she lingers and weeps.

"Woman, why are you weeping? Whom are you looking for?" It's the voice of Jesus, whom she mistakes for the gardener.

At hearing him utter her name, she recognizes who he is— another literary gem pointing to a spiritual truth. She would embrace him but he sends her on a mission. "Go and tell my brothers that I am risen."

Ladies and gents, meet Mary Magdalene, the first apostle of the resurrection. Jesus sends her off to proclaim it to those still entombed in the culture of death. The shame his culture heaps on women is no deterrent to Jesus. He grants her the honor now of liberating the entombed.

That evening Jesus appears to the community locked away in hiding. "Peace be with you" are his first words. Then after showing them the wounds of his crucifixion, he says again: "Peace be with you." John is pressing a point—a startling point, so he presses it obliquely. He's telling us that the peace Jesus offers is contingent on his wounds. Resurrection peace comes by way of nonviolently resisting the culture of death. Shortly put, by risking the cross. More startling yet, he passes the mantle on. "As the Father sent me, so I send you." And he breathes on them— "Receive the Holy Spirit"—and then confers on them soaring authority. "Those whom you forgive, are forgiven. Those you hold in community are retained." An authority vastly different than that of emperors and rulers. Here Jesus confers authority to reconcile. With these words he sends them into the chaotic world of violence to build communities of nonviolence, a mission passed down through the ages to ourselves.

Now we are to live together in the spirit of *agape* and peace, as servants of life, as proclaimers of the resurrection and all its social, economic, and political implications, understanding full well that Jesus' resurrection was illegal, knowing that it portends the undoing of empire because it robs the state of its only intimidation—the threat of death. We are to trust and proclaim. Death has no more sway; it is struck from empire's hands. It is not something to fear but to defy.

Little do we realize: the resurrection of Jesus is the ultimate revolution.

And a gentle revolution at that. Jesus returns to his tortured land, to the disciples who had scattered, not like Zeus or Mars fulminating in anger, not seeking revenge, but bearing the gift of peace. He exacts no retribution; there is no hell to pay. Neither does he unleash a riot of vengeance on the Temple or Rome. How unlike the gods of war. How unlike you and me, who can nurse grudges for decades.

None of that. No trace of condemnation. He had declared to Pilate that God's kingdom rejects violence. Then he proved it on the cross and now again before his disciples. He forgives them, offers them even now his steadfast love. More, he banishes hierarchy. Lordliness bows to friendship: Jesus shows himself to be their friend.

On the shore of the Sea of Galilee, he makes them breakfast. It's a touching, intimate scene. The disciples, having gone back to their livelihoods, pull into shore. Then we read: "When it was dawn, there on the shore stood Jesus." Waiting for them, looking forward to their return. The sentence is simple but brims with camaraderie and welcome. From the boat, with the sun rising, the disciples strain to make out his dark form in the distance. A beautiful new day, an image of peace, hope, and love. The risen Jesus stands silhouetted against a rising sun. He waits for them, and us.

A "charcoal fire" crackles nearby. And he invites them gently, "Come, have breakfast." They eat in silence, none daring "to ask who he was."

And here, I think, is the font of resurrection peace. Silence, a common meal, the risen Jesus present, the beauty of creation. I like to imagine the scene and place myself in the circle. There, in my prayerful imagining, I sense Jesus' peaceful presence and the soothing of my battered soul. In that intimate circle I feel new beginnings of love, hope, peace, even joy.

I urge you to try this. Conjure holy settings as you read them; let them be the context for forming your own peaceful life. From those spiritual settings, we too can go into the world of violence on a mission of liberation to lead humanity from its tombs.

It was certainly a new beginning for Simon Peter. As Jesus suffered torture, Peter disavowed any knowledge of him in front of the empire's "charcoal fire." Now he sits and eats before Christ's "charcoal fire."

He had denied knowing Jesus three times; now three times Jesus poses the question: "Simon Peter, do you love me?" Three times: "Do you *agapao* me?" And three times: "Yes, Lord. You know that I *phileo* you." (*Phileo*: "brotherly love.") Nonetheless, Jesus and Simon Peter are reconciled. And for the first time Jesus explicitly calls his impetuous friend to the life of nonviolence. "Simon Peter, follow me."

Jesus has risen, and he stands beyond all cultures of violence and war and above psychological urges toward rancor and ill will. In his gentle reunion he demonstrates nothing but *agape*, compassion, kindness, reconciliation, peace, and joy. And it transforms their hearts. We know this from the book of Acts. Upon Jesus' ascension, they take to the streets, form communities, confront injustice publicly, and offer their lives to embody Jesus' vision.

This is what the resurrection of Jesus has in store for us, as well. He calls us out of tombs of our own making and into the freedom of nonviolence. When we step into freedom we will, like the early community, have nothing to do with death anymore. We will not join the armed forces or fail to decry executions or make our livings in industries that design weapons. We will not make wealth our pursuit or hoard more than we need. We will not be violent to ourselves or to anyone. We will be nonviolent people offering the world compassion, *agape*, and peace.

Life is short, but our survival is guaranteed. So we can risk living in solidarity with all, especially the forsaken and even the enemies imposed on us by our nation. We can live life to the full, and so resist the forces of death, knowing that our resurrection has already begun.

This is the key to fullness of life here and now. And it's a foretaste of eternity, at home in Jesus' circle, at peace with creation, our hearts healed in the aura of his love. This is our invitation to forsake the wiles of death and live life to the full.

Now we know it's true: *The kingdom of God is life.*

CONCLUSION

The Gospel of John presents a stunning illustration of how the God of life enters the culture of death and calls humanity out of the tombs into the new life of resurrection. If we can begin to understand this climactic parable in the life and works of Jesus as a story of God's action to liberate all humanity in the figure of the dead Lazarus, then we have been given a great mission—to join God's campaign to lead humanity to the fullness of life.

This great text summons us to obey the three new commandments of Jesus. We are told to "Take away the stone" that keeps us all entombed in the old ways of death, such as war, violence, greed, and injustice. We hear ourselves called out of the tomb with a bold summons from the God of life, "Lazarus, come forth!" We join that voice by calling one another to come forth out of the culture of war and death into new life. And we are commanded, "Unbind him and let him go free!" With that final commandment, we are sent to unbind humanity from the trappings of death and injustice, that every human being may live free in dignity, love, and peace to follow Jesus on the path into new life.

This Gospel story sets the path for the rest of our lives. We are no longer dead, but summoned to live life to the full. That means, we have to renounce our complicity with the culture of death, and do what we can to help everyone else live life to the full.

At this tumultuous hour in our history, Jesus' invitation offers astounding new hope. He empowers us to do what we can not only to liberate humanity from the powers of death, but to transform the culture itself into a new culture of justice, nonviolence, peace, and life. To do that, we need to join local, national, and global grassroots movements for nonviolent social change. Like the Abolitionists of old, we announce an improbable, nearly impossible dream—the abolition of war, poverty, nuclear weapons, and violence of every kind. We summon everyone into the new life of nonviolence, the new life of resurrection peace, the fullness of life which is God's Kingdom here in our midst.

We can go forward now, filled with hope, knowing that our God is a God of life who wants us to live life to the full, that our resurrection has already begun, that the days of the culture of death are already over.

May the God of life and peace give us strength for the task ahead, and make us instruments of resurrection peace. Amen. Alleluia.

QUESTIONS FOR PERSONAL REFLECTION AND SMALL GROUP DISCUSSION

1. What does Jesus mean when he says that he has come to bring us "the fullness of life"? Do we want to live life to the full? How do we live life to the full? How is our world, instead, a culture of death? In what ways are we comfortable with the culture of violence, war, and death?

2. Is Jesus nonviolent, and if so, what does that mean for us individually as his followers and collectively for the church? How do we journey with Jesus from violence to nonviolence, reject the ways of the culture of death, and follow Jesus on the path of life?

3. How does Jesus confront the culture of death? How can we publicly confront the culture of violence, war and death?

4. Where do you see yourselves in the story of John, chapter 11? In the male disciples? In the professional mourners? In Martha and Mary? In Lazarus? In Jesus?

5. In what ways are we, like Martha, "disappointed" with God? When have we said, "Lord, if you had only been

here . . . ?" What does Jesus say to us in return? When has Jesus said to us, "Your brother, your sister, will rise?" How do we respond to his talk of resurrection?

6.   What does this statement by Jesus mean to you: "I am the resurrection and the life. Whoever believes in me, even if he or she dies, will live, and everyone who lives and believes in me will never die?" How do we respond when Jesus asks, "Do you believe this?"

7.   How do you imagine this verse: "Jesus approached the tomb"? How does Jesus approach the tomb, the culture of war and death, today? How do we?

8.   How do you fulfill the first commandment: "Take away the stone!"? When have you rolled away the stone from the culture of death? Do you want the stone rolled away? How do you, like Martha, resist this commandment? What is "the stench" that happens today when we confront the culture of death?

9.   Do you pray like Martha or Jesus? How often do you give thanks like Jesus? Do you thank God for the nonviolent movements that take away the stone from the culture of death today? How can we thank the God of life more and more for this work of liberation?

10. How do you fulfill the second commandment: "Lazarus, come forth!"? How is Jesus calling you out of the tomb, the culture of violence, war, and death? How do you call others out of the tomb, the culture of violence, war, and death?

11. Where do you see humanity rising, and coming out of the tomb, the culture of violence, war, and death, today?

12. How do you fulfill the third commandment: "Unbind him and let him go free!"? Who unbinds you and sets you free? What people in the world are bound and not free because of the culture of death? How can we unbind them and set them free?

13. What inspires you and challenges you in the stories of Ben Salmon, Dorothy Stang, and Oscar Romero?

14. How do we "wash each other's feet," that is, prepare one another to walk the way of the cross as nonviolent resistance to injustice and the culture of war and death? Who washed your feet? Whose feet do you wash?

15. How do we give our lives in *agape*/love for one another and humanity? How do we practice resurrection and welcome the risen Jesus' gift of peace here and now?

16. What gives you hope these days? How does the nonviolent Jesus and the Gospel of life give you hope? What hopeful things for peace and justice do you do, can you do?

17. What can we do to help abolish war, poverty, starvation, executions, nuclear weapons, and environmental destruction? How do we live life in the Kingdom of God here and now?

About the Author

John Dear is an internationally recognized voice for peace and nonviolence. A priest, pastor, peacemaker, retreat leader, and author, he served for years as the director of the Fellowship of Reconciliation, the largest interfaith peace organization in the United States. After September 11, 2001, he worked with the Red Cross as a coordinator of chaplains at the Family Assistance Center in New York and counseled thousands of relatives and rescue workers. He has traveled the war zones of the world, been arrested some seventy-five times in civil disobedience against war and injustice, led Nobel Peace Prize winners to Iraq, given thousands of lectures on peace across the United States, and served as pastor to several churches in the desert of New Mexico. He writes a weekly column for the *National Catholic Reporter* at *www.ncronline.org.* Recently, Archbishop Desmond Tutu nominated John Dear for the Nobel Peace Prize.

John Dear's many books include *The God of Peace; Transfiguration; You Will Be My Witnesses; Living Peace; The Questions of Jesus; Put Down Your Sword; Jesus the Rebel; Peace behind Bars; Disarming the Heart; Seeds of Nonviolence; Daniel Berrigan: Essential Writings; Mohandas Gandhi: Essential Writings; The Sound of Listening;* and his recent autobiography, *A Persistent Peace.* He is featured in the DVD film *The Narrow Path.*

For information see *www.johndear.org.*

179